IN THE COCKPIT II

IN THE COCKPIT II

INSIDE HISTORY-MAKING AIRCRAFT OF WORLD WAR II

PHOTOGRAPHY BY ERIC F. LONG AND MARK A. AVINO

TEXT BY ROGER D. CONNOR AND CHRISTOPHER T. MOORE

FOREWORD BY ROBERT A. HOOVER

COLLINS DESIGN

An Imprint of HarperCollinsPublishers

IN ASSOCIATION WITH

THE NATIONAL AIR AND SPACE MUSEUM,
SMITHSONIAN INSTITUTION

In the Cockpit II: Inside History-Making Aircraft of World War II
Copyright © 2010 by the SMITHSONIAN INSTITUTION

HarperCollins books may be purchased for educational, business, or sales promotional use.
For information, please write: Special Markets Department, HarperCollins Publishers,
10 East 53rd Street, New York, NY 10022.

An Imprint of HarperCollins*Publishers*
10 East 53rd Street
New York, NY 10022
Tel: (212) 207-7000
Fax: (212) 207-7654
collinsdesign@harpercollins.com
www.harpercollins.com

Distributed throughout the world by:
HarperCollins*Publishers*
10 East 53rd Street
New York, NY 10022
Fax: (212) 207-7654

Designed by Agnieszka Stachowicz

Library of Congress Control Number: 2009934047

ISBN 978-0-06-168434-0

Printed in China
First Printing 2010

This book is dedicated to Donald S. Lopez* and those aircrew, ground crew, and engineers who supported the air war against the Axis tyrannies that threatened freedom in the terrifyingly tumultuous years from 1939 to 1945. The images presented here are a testament to the skill and fortitude of these extraordinary people and their opponents.

*Lieutenant Colonel Lopez (USAF, Ret.) was an ace with the Twenty-third Fighter Group, Fourteenth Air Force in China and served as deputy director of the National Air and Space Museum until his passing in 2008. He is sorely missed.

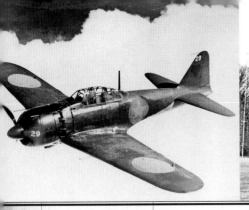

FOREWORD

From the first storm clouds over Europe to the surrender of Japan, military cockpits saw dramatic improvements, yet by present-day comparisons they seem primitive. Having flown many of the planes depicted in this book, including most of the captured enemy aircraft, evaluating them on speed, altitude, range, and turning radius, I am often asked, "Which was the best fighter over Europe?"

This very same question was posed to a gathering of World War II fighter aces, and each pilot responded with the name of the aircraft type he flew in his Fighter Group. Colonel Hubert "Hub" Zemke, one of the most renowned P–47 aces, was the last pilot to be questioned, and his remarks surprised everyone. He asked his fellow aces how many of them had been in combat in two or more types of fighter types. Only two responded. Hub then stated, "Gentlemen, I have flown combat with all of your fighters and commanded each type of Fighter Group and I can assure you the P–51, with its ideal balance of maneuverability, performance, firepower, and range, was the best of them all." This is my answer as well.

I wish to extend my appreciation to Gen. Jack Dailey (USMC, Ret.), Eric Long, Mark Avino, Chris Moore, and Roger Connor for this pictorial history of fading, but not forgotten, memories of yesteryear.

—ROBERT A. "BOB" HOOVER

PHOTOGRAPHER'S NOTE

As we enter our third book of cockpit interiors, we do so with large megabyte digital capture replacing large format film. This is due in part to the difficulty of getting film processed, the demise of Polaroid Instant proofing film, and to some degree, the difficulty of working with a film camera inside the cockpit. We advanced from shooting 4 x 5 films to working on the same Cambo Wide DS camera format, but adapted for a Phase One P-45 digital back, producing a 112 megabyte file size. The camera is supplied with a 24mm XL lens and center grade filter, giving the equivalent coverage of a 17mm lens on a 35mm camera.

Digital enabled us to view the image immediately on a laptop to check composition, lighting and focus. Due to the lack of a dedicated system, the camera and lens operated separately from the digital back, which needed a prestart before capturing an image. This required extra-long cabling attached to and from the computer and digital back and a cable release to the camera. The computer would not fire the camera, thus the shutter had to be manually cocked and fired. This could be accomplished by the person at the computer, or by someone inside the plane.

The digital files are shot in a RAW format. This allowed us the capabilities of working from one file to maintain shadow and highlight detail. It is to some degree like bracketing exposures on film. I prefer lighting as if we were shooting film, believing that digital manipulation should be a last resort. There are two downsides to digital. First, it is virtually impossible to enlarge a cropped area within a file to reproduction quality. Second, there is the issue of archiving the digital file. With film, it can be viewed years from now to determine what it is. With digital capture, it remains to be seen what media the image will be stored on and how it will eventually be viewed by future generations.

—ERIC F. LONG

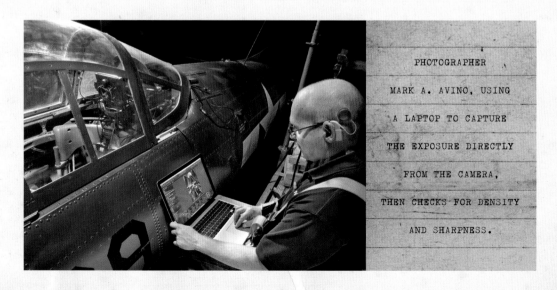

PHOTOGRAPHER MARK A. AVINO, USING A LAPTOP TO CAPTURE THE EXPOSURE DIRECTLY FROM THE CAMERA, THEN CHECKS FOR DENSITY AND SHARPNESS.

AUTHORS' NOTE

World War II occurred as aeronautical technology was undergoing a significant transformation. Though many new technologies, such as jet and rocket propulsion, radar, and helicopters were emerging before the outbreak of war, the unprecedented flow of government funds for research, development, testing, and production resulted in a dizzying transformation of the pilot's environment in just a few years. The following pages reveal a wide range of complexity and ingenuity as seen on 34 aircraft operated by the major combatants during World War II. These aircraft reside today in the collection of the Smithsonian's National Air and Space Museum. Some examples, such as the Aichi Seiran, have seen at least a decade of meticulous restoration to overcome the ravages of time. Others, such as the Bell Kingcobra, have weathered the years well with no intervention whatsoever. The Kyushu Shinden illustrates another group that is in desperate need of restoration and looks it. While several aircraft, like the *Enola Gay*, have been restored to a specific wartime moment (August 6, 1945), the Northrop Black Widow and Martin Mariner represent aircraft that continued their service well beyond the war years and whose cockpits reflect postwar modifications.

Many of the aircraft seen herein are on display, either at the Smithsonian's flagship museum complex on the National Mall in Washington, D.C., or at the spectacular Steven F. Udvar-Hazy Center located in Chantilly, Virginia. A number of the aircraft are in storage awaiting restoration at the Paul E. Garber Preservation, Restoration, and Storage Facility in Suitland, Maryland. Several examples are on loan to other museums around the nation. These aircraft represent only a portion of the extensive World War II collection at the National Air and Space Museum. Some examples were excluded because of their inclusion in the previous volume of *In the Cockpit* or because of condition or lack of accessibility.

For many years, we have had the privilege to work around the exteriors of these aircraft. Preparing this book has given us a new appreciation for those who designed, built, and flew these incredible machines. We hope that beyond enjoying the sheer artistry of Eric and Mark's photographs, you will come away with just a little more understanding of what it was like to fly in those turbulent times.

—ROGER D. CONNOR AND CHRISTOPHER T. MOORE

AICHI M6A1 SEIRAN

Situated half a world away from the United States, Japan's geographic isolation influenced its war-fighting approach and led to the pursuit of unorthodox naval technologies, including a series of submarine-launched combat aircraft. The Seiran (Clear Sky Storm) was the final and most capable of these designs but was never used in combat. In the aftermath of the Doolittle Raid on Tokyo and subsequent losses during the Battle of Midway, the value of a submarine aircraft carrier with strike aircraft became more apparent. Japan already had extensive experience with submarine-launched aircraft, but in spite of a notable (if unsuccessful) 1942 bombing raid against the Oregon coast, these planes were designed for scouting, not bombing. By late 1942, the Aichi Company was developing the M6A1 as a true strike aircraft with a bomb or torpedo load of 800 kilograms. Accommodating several Seiran aircraft required construction of new submarines of unprecedented size. Work began on the I–400 class submarine with a cruising range of 20,000 miles and the capacity to accommodate three M6A1s in a special 12-foot diameter watertight hangar tube. The similar I–13 class could accommodate two Seirans.

Folding wings and stabilizers facilitated stowage. Crews could deploy and launch the submarine's full complement of three Seirans in less than 30 minutes using a catapult built into the forward deck. The Seiran operated with floats as a reconnaissance aircraft, but the crew dispensed with them for strike missions; if not undertaking a kamikaze (special attack) mission, the aircraft would ditch near the sub on its return.

In June 1945, the I–13, I–14, I–400, and I–401 submarines were to launch their 10 aircraft in kamikaze attacks against a crucial Panama Canal lock. Before this plan was executed, the Japanese High Command decided that the U.S. naval forces assembling at Ulithi Atoll were a greater threat. The Seirans were repainted in American markings in an attempt to foil the extensive defenses of the anchorage and were nearing the launch area when the war ended.

Despite the unusual mission of the aircraft, the cockpit is consistent with other Japanese naval strike aircraft. What appears to be a gunsight atop the instrument panel is actually a bombsight. A similar looking component in the front of the navigator/gunner's station is an aperiodic compass with reflector. The orange cones are speaking tubes. This aircraft is the sole surviving example of a Seiran.

THE SEIRAN COULD BE LAUNCHED WITHOUT FLOATS FOR KAMIKAZE MISSIONS.

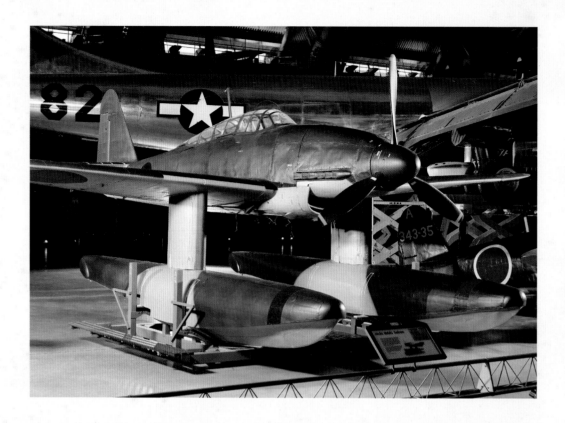

ABOVE: THE SOLE SURVIVING SEIRAN ON DISPLAY AT THE STEVEN F. UDVAR-HAZY CENTER.

BOTTOM: THE IMPERIAL JAPANESE NAVY BEGAN CONSTRUCTION ON FIVE I-400 CLASS SUBMARINES, BUT WAS ONLY ABLE TO COMPLETE THREE, AND ONE OF THOSE FAILED TO MAKE IT INTO OPERATION.

RIGHT: NAVIGATOR/GUNNER'S POSITION LOOKING FORWARD.

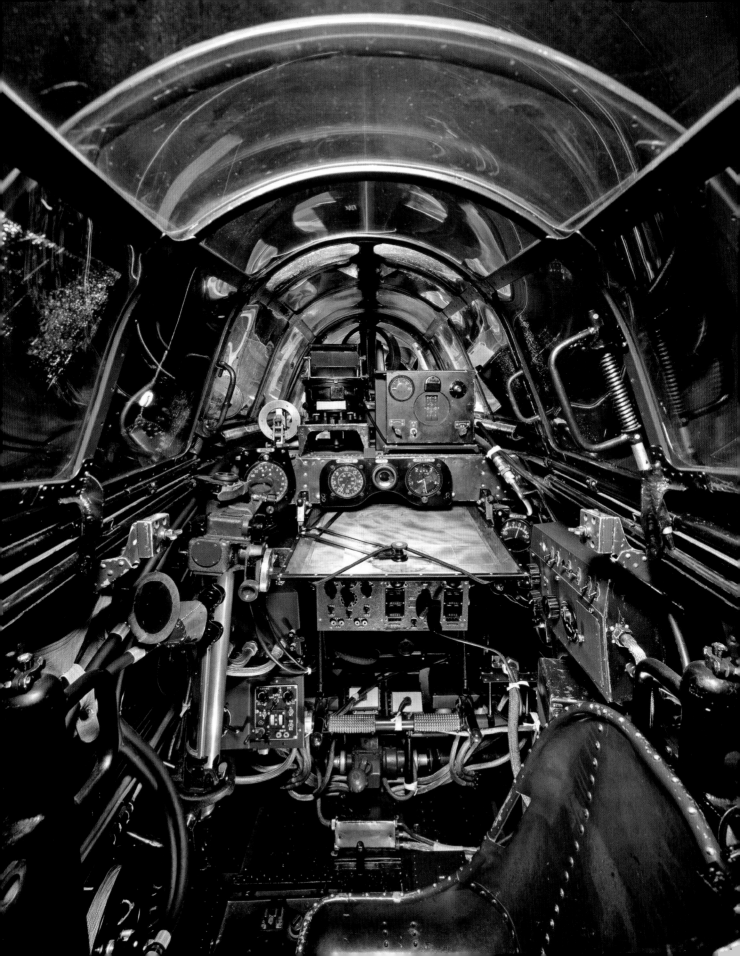

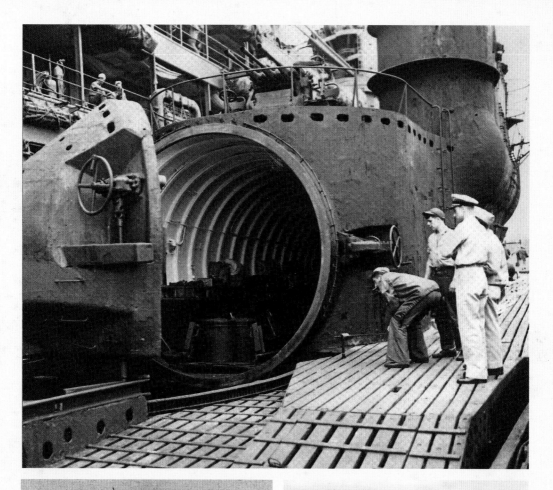

ABOVE: THE I-400'S HANGAR
WAS A LARGE WATERTIGHT
TUBE MOUNTED ON TOP OF
THE MAIN HULL.

RIGHT: A CATAPULT BUILT
INTO THE DECK ALLOWED
LAUNCHING OF THE SEIRAN,
WITH OR WITHOUT FLOATS.

LEFT: NAVIGATOR/GUNNER'S
POSITION LOOKING AFT OVER THE
13MM TYPE 2 MACHINE GUN.

ARADO AR 234 B-2 BLITZ

In late 1940, the Reichsluftfahrtministerium (German Air Ministry) issued a requirement for a turbojet-powered reconnaissance aircraft. Arado designed a sleek, high-wing aircraft with two Jumo 004 engines. A shortage of engines prevented the Arado prototype from flying until 1943 and from entering service until after D-Day. Nonetheless, it was still the world's first operational jet reconnaissance aircraft and bomber.

The prototype used a jettisonable trolley for takeoff to reduce weight and provide space for extra fuel. The shortcomings of this system were soon realized, and production versions featured a widened fuselage with a tricycle landing gear and a semirecessed bomb bay. An autopilot was installed to control the aircraft while the pilot concentrated on operating the bombsight. Droppable Walther 109–500 Rocket-Assisted Takeoff (RATO) motors were mounted under the wing to shorten the type's agonizingly long takeoff roll.

The extensive glazing of the nose of the Blitz (Lightning) provided the pilot with an excellent forward view. Flight instruments were mounted so as to provide as little visual interference as possible. The control yoke was mounted to the side so that in the bombing run it could be pivoted away. The PDS autopilot would first be set with the control mounted on the right handle of the yoke. Then the controls were swung to the side and the pilot could lean forward and look through the bombsight located between his knees. The instruments in the cockpits of most German aircraft used a color- and letter-coding system so that aircrew could quickly identify systems. The yellow fuel indicators are prominent. Near the top of the cockpit is the sight for the rearward-looking RF2C periscope. Originally designed to sight a pair of guns mounted in the tail that were never installed, and to serve as a dive-bombing sight, it was used operationally to spot fighters approaching from the rear, particularly during the Blitz's vulnerable approach to landing.

In August 1944, one of the prototypes made the first operational reconnaissance flights over the Normandy front where its speed and altitude allowed it to operate with relative impunity. The principle unit to use the type, KG76, also operated the aircraft as a bomber, but it was marginal in this role. The unreliability of the Jumo engines and a lack of fuel in the closing months of the war limited the usefulness of this excellent aircraft. This example, the sole surviving Ar 234, served with KG76 in Norway.

THE SOLE SURVIVING AR 234 ON DISPLAY AT THE UDVAR-HAZY CENTER.

BELL P-39Q AIRACOBRA
GALLOPING GERTIE

With over 7,500 examples built, the P–39 was one of the principle American fighters constructed during World War II, yet its legacy is one of an innovative but troubled aircraft that operated in the shadow of higher performance counterparts, such as the P–51. Bell's 1937 design incorporated a liquid-cooled in-line engine mounted behind the cockpit, tricycle landing gear, and automobile-style doors in place of a sliding canopy. Unfortunately, nearly all of these features put it at a disadvantage. The Allison V–1710 engine lacked a turbo-supercharger, severely hobbling its ability to fight at altitude and its aft center of gravity caused by the engine placement made it unpredictable in stalls and spins. Pilots also disliked bailing out of the awkward side doors. The weight of the heavy tricycle gear and long driveshaft limited fuel capacity. On the other hand, the P–39 was very maneuverable and relatively fast. It also packed a heavy punch in armament, typically mounting a 37 mm cannon fired through the propeller hub, twin .50 caliber machine guns in the nose, and two additional .50 caliber machine guns in underwing pods.

In American service, P–39s flew operations in secondary combat areas, such as the Mediterranean, New Guinea, and the Aleutians, where they enjoyed moderate success against enemy aircraft. Britain's Royal Air Force found them unsuited to combat, though the Soviet Union made great use of them and the majority of Airacobra production went to the Soviets under the Lend-Lease Act. Contrary to mythology, the Soviets preferred the Airacobra for its dogfighting qualities rather than its capability in the ground attack role, and a number of their pilots became aces in the type.

This example served in the latter part of the war training replacement pilots. Postwar, it had a brief career as an air racer. Pilot Elizabeth Haas had it painted red and white, named it *Galloping Gertie*, and, in 1948, tried to enter it in the National Air Races, but failed to qualify.

The most obvious indication of the aircraft's air-racing heritage is the removal of the .50 caliber machine guns, whose breeches dominated the upper left and right sides of the instrument panel. Otherwise, Haas and a previous civil owner kept nearly the entire original military configuration intact. Haas appears to have scrawled a number of power settings and configuration notes around the panel.

IF NOT A SUPERB DOGFIGHTER, THE P-39 AT LEAST PACKED A HEAVY PUNCH IN ARMAMENT.

BELL P-63A KINGCOBRA
EDYTH LOUISE

In the months before Pearl Harbor, the P-63 was born out of the rapid movement to establish the Army Air Corps on a war-capable footing and was an attempt to improve upon some of the less desirable traits of the Bell P-39 Airacobra. Though quite similar in exterior appearance to its predecessor, the Kingcobra featured a lengthened fuselage and wings, along with a considerably upgraded version of the Allison V-1710 and, perhaps most important, a two-stage supercharger to overcome the P-39's inadequate performance at higher altitudes.

Development and production proceeded slowly for an aircraft that was largely an enhancement of an existing design, and the P-63 was not ready for operational deployment until late 1943. By that time, better performing P-38s, P-47s, and P-51s were already gaining the upper hand over the Luftwaffe. The Kingcobra's limited fuel capacity made it unsuitable for deployment to the Pacific combat theater. Thus, the Army Air Forces was left with an underperforming aircraft in full-scale production, which would ultimately result in the creation of 3,273 unwanted aircraft. The obvious solution was to use the P-63s in support of Lend-Lease requests—the bulk of the deliveries going to the Soviet Union and a small number to France. Only during the Soviet invasion of Japanese-held Manchuria in the closing days of the war did the P-63 finally see combat. The most notable American use of the P-63 occurred during Operation Pinball, in which P-63s with additional heavy armor plating flew as targets for aerial gunnery trainees using frangible bullets designed to shatter on impact.

This P-63A served principally as a cold-weather test and evaluation aircraft in Alaska in the later months of World War II. Given that it had no postwar career, it is complete and well preserved, having undergone no significant restoration.

The Kingcobra's cockpit is similar to the Airacobra's, but shows a more refined panel design. The two red-bounded buttons on the right of the panel detonated small charges in the SCR 695-A IFF (Identification Friend or Foe) radio to deny them to the enemy in the event of a forced landing. The large crank on the front right of the seat manually extended the gear in the event of hydraulic failure. The smaller red handles in the center of the doors rolled down the windows as in an automobile. Missing from the top center of the panel is the N-9 gunsight.

P-63 FIRING DEMONSTRATION AT NIGHT.

BOEING B–17G FLYING FORTRESS
SHOO SHOO SHOO BABY

The Flying Fortress shaped the air war over Western Europe like no other aircraft. From the outset of combat, it provided a strategic bombing capability that the Axis could never match. Its long-range, heavy payload, lethal defensive armament, and rugged construction allowed the Army Air Forces to pursue a strategy of unescorted daylight precision bombing over heavily defended targets in Western Europe. While the strategic bombing campaign suffered its share of missteps and the legacy of civilian casualties is still hotly debated, the efficacy of the Flying Fortress in crippling German industry and infrastructure is not in doubt. Eighth Air Force B–17s alone dropped well over 400,000 tons of bombs on Axis-held territory from August 17, 1942, to May 8, 1945. However, 4,754 Flying Fortresses were lost or written off in the course of operations, constituting 37 percent of the production run of 12,731 airframes.

Boeing built its prototype Model 299 to a 1934 Air Corps specification for a bomber with a 2,000-lb bomb load and a radius of action of more than 1,000 miles. By 1940, the B–17, as it had come to be designated, had evolved into a capable combat aircraft. The American heavy bomber doctrine that evolved through the 1930s centered on daylight precision bombing, though in operations "precision" would be a relative term, with Eighth Air Force heavy bombers dropping 50 percent of their bombs more than 1,500

THE *SHOO SHOO SHOO BABY* ON DISPLAY AT THE NATIONAL MUSEUM OF THE U.S. AIR FORCE.

ITS WARTIME PAINT SCHEME WAS UNPAINTED BARE METAL.

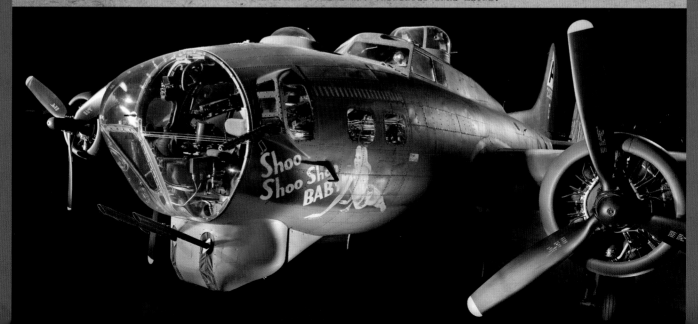

feet from their targets. The solution was to fly larger formations, putting even more aircraft under the guns of capable German fighters. B–17 armament proliferated with later models mounting up to 13 .50 caliber machine guns and carrying a crew of 10. The defensive fire of B–17s took its toll on the Luftwaffe attackers, but the survival of these formations would ultimately depend on the ability of escorts to minimize the exposure to German air defense fighters.

Shoo Shoo Shoo Baby is one of the only surviving B–17Gs with a combat record. It entered service with the Ninety-first Bomb Group in March 1943. On May 29, 1944, after an extensive period of combat, the aircraft departed for a raid on the Focke-Wulf plant in Poznan, Poland. After its bomb run, the aircraft suffered flak damage and was forced to land in neutral Sweden, where the aircraft was interned with its crew. The Swedish government sold the aircraft to SAAB, who turned the Flying Fortress into an airliner. The U.S. Air Force later rescued the aircraft after it had been abandoned and eventually undertook a massive program to restore it.

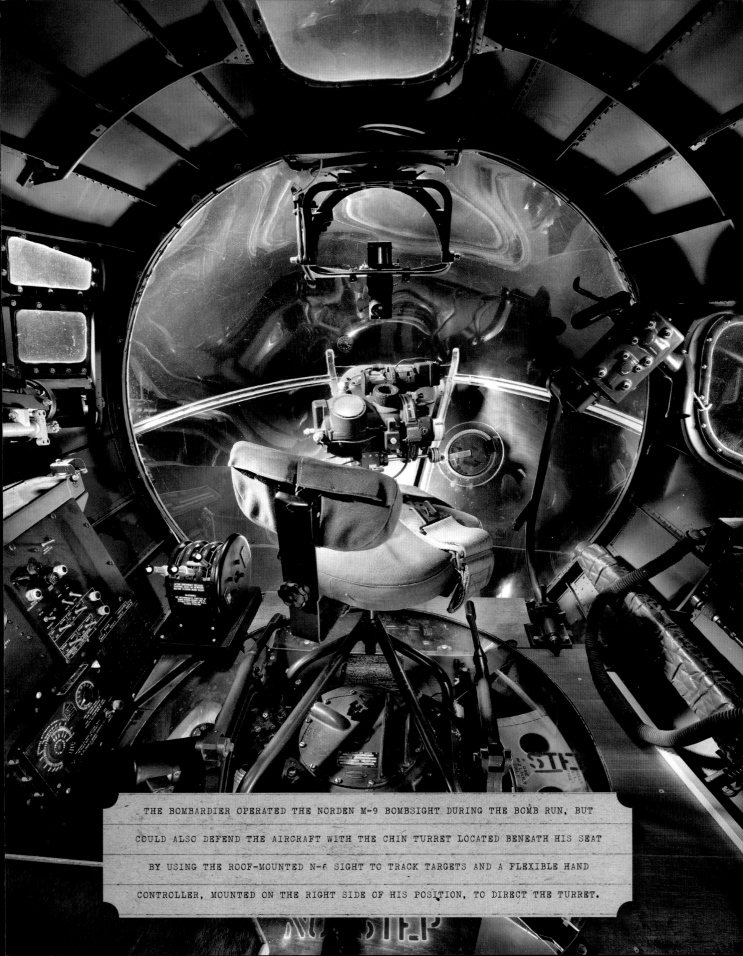

THE BOMBARDIER OPERATED THE NORDEN M-9 BOMBSIGHT DURING THE BOMB RUN, BUT
COULD ALSO DEFEND THE AIRCRAFT WITH THE CHIN TURRET LOCATED BENEATH HIS SEAT
BY USING THE ROOF-MOUNTED N-6 SIGHT TO TRACK TARGETS AND A FLEXIBLE HAND
CONTROLLER, MOUNTED ON THE RIGHT SIDE OF HIS POSITION, TO DIRECT THE TURRET.

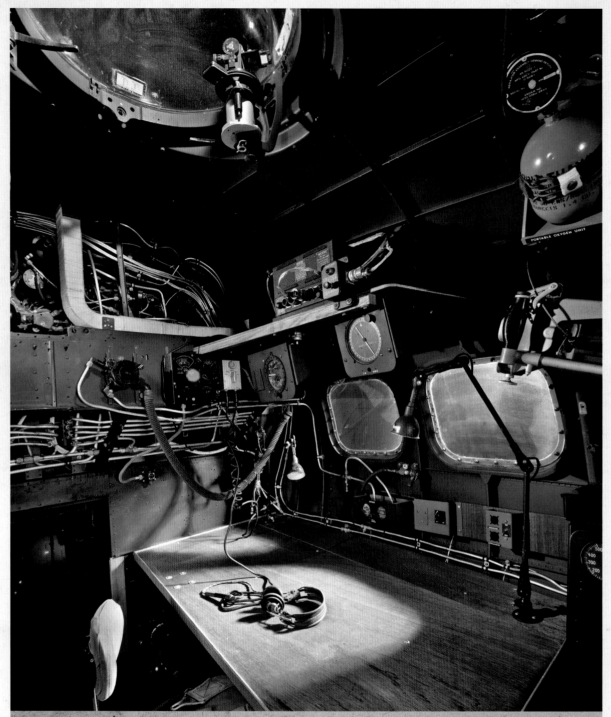

COMPARED WITH THE B-29, THE B-17'S NAVIGATION EQUIPMENT WAS BASIC. THE NAVIGATOR'S PRINCIPLE TOOLS WERE THE AIR POSITION INDICATOR (AN ELECTROMECHANICAL DEAD RECKONING COMPUTER), A DRIFT SIGHT, AND AN ASTRODOME TO TAKE SEXTANT SIGHTINGS. THE NAVIGATOR COULD ALSO ASSIST THE BOMBARDIER IN FENDING OFF DEADLY HEAD-ON ATTACKS BY MANNING THE TWO ANM2 .50 CALIBER MACHINE GUNS MOUNTED ON EITHER SIDE OF THE NOSE.

THE RADIO OPERATOR EMPLOYED A RANGE OF LIAISON AND

COMMAND RADIO SETS IN THE COURSE OF HIS COMMMUNICATIONS

DUTIES AND TUNED IN ELECTRONIC ASSEMBLY

BEACONS AND LANDING AIDS TO ASSIST WITH NAVIGATION.

THE RADIO OPERATOR MANNED HIS RELATIVELY

SPACIOUS POSITION BETWEEN

THE BOMB BAY AND THE WAIST GUN COMPARTMENT. LOOKING AFT,

HE COULD SEE THE TOP OF THE BALL TURRET.

ONE OF THE MOST GRUELING ASSIGNMENTS IN THE AIR WAR WAS THAT OF THE BALL

TURRET GUNNER. THE GUNNER ENTERED THE CRAMPED TURRET AFTER TAKEOFF BY

ROTATING THE GUNS DOWNWARD. UNLESS TRACKING A TARGET, THE GUNNER RECLINED ON

HIS BACK WITH THE GUNS PARALLEL TO THE FUSELAGE.

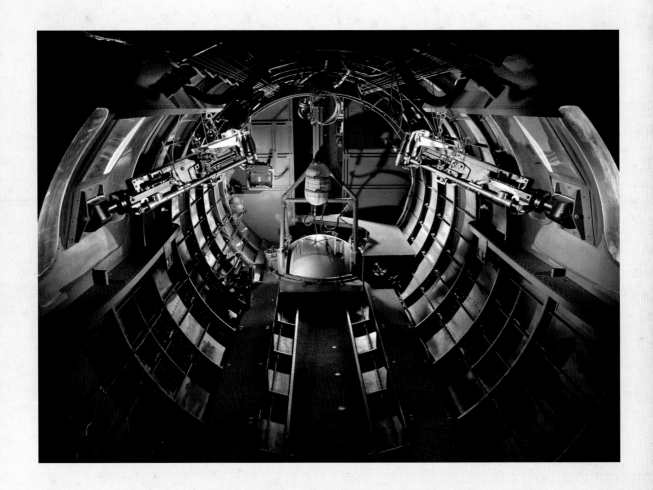

ABOVE: MANNING THE WAIST GUNS WAS UNCOMFORTABLE AND HAZARDOUS. OPERATING AT ALTITUDES

UP TO 25,000 FEET IN AN UNPRESSURIZED CABIN, TEMPERATURES OFTEN PLUNGED TO MINUS 60

DEGREES FAHRENHEIT. FROSTBITE, HYPOXIA, AND THE CHALLENGE OF OPERATING IN BULKY FLIGHT

GEAR AND FLAK JACKETS MADE AIMING AND FIRING THE GUNS A CONSTANT CHALLENGE.

RIGHT: THE NATURE OF BOMBER INTERCEPTION MADE THE TAIL OF THE AIRCRAFT A FREQUENT

TARGET AND THE B-17 TAIL GUNNER HAD TO TRUST IN THE ARMOR PLATE IN FRONT OF

HIS KNEELING POSITION TO PROTECT HIM.

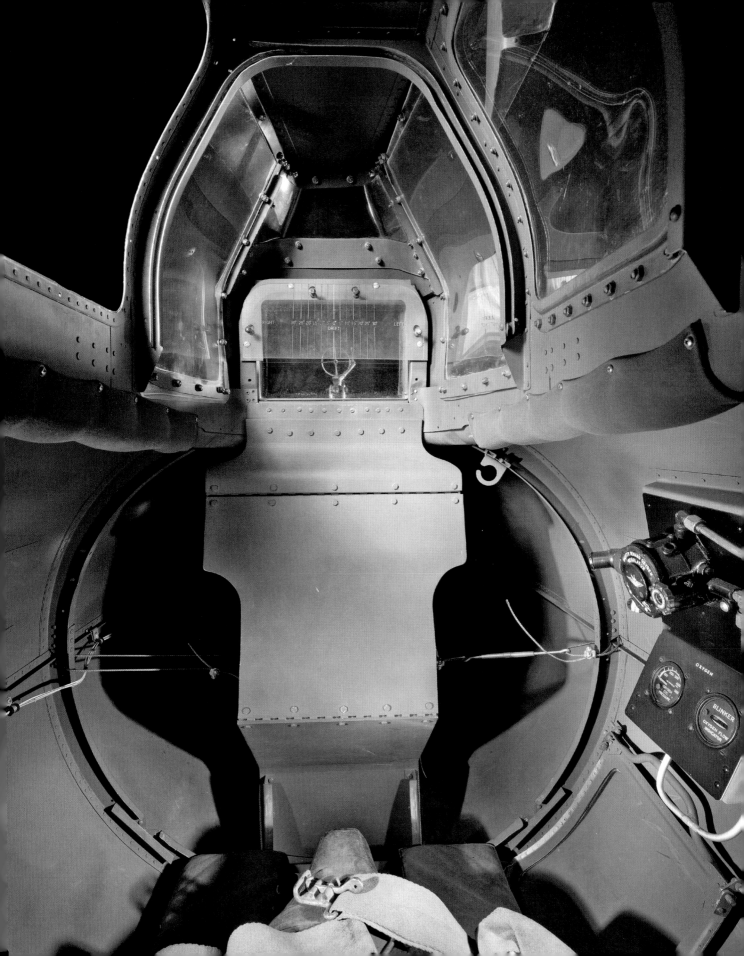

ABOVE: THE *ENOLA GAY* UPON COMPLETION OF ITS 12-HOUR, 13-MINUTE MISSION TO HIROSHIMA.

LEFT: TO DROP THE *LITTLE BOY* ATOMIC BOMB, MAJ. THOMAS FEREBEE USED A STANDARD NORDEN M-9B
BOMBSIGHT COUPLED TO THE PILOTS' C-1 AUTOPILOT TO LOCK IN THE AIM POINT IN CENTRAL HIROSHIMA.

BOEING B-29 SUPER-FORTRESS *ENOLA GAY*

Of all the World War II aircraft in the collection of the National Air and Space Museum, the most significant is the *Enola Gay*. On August 6, 1945, in the first combat use of the atomic bomb, this Army Air Forces Superfortress from the 509th Composite Group dropped the 13-kiloton *Little Boy* on the Japanese city of Hiroshima, decimating it. Even after the passage of six decades, its role in ending the war and the morality of the atomic bombings continue to be hotly debated. However, there is no endeavor that better illustrates the unprecedented commitment and national investment in combating America's totalitarian enemies than the pairing of the B-29 and the Manhattan Project that developed the atomic bomb.

The results of these programs had implications far beyond the devastation they wrought in the Pacific. They forever altered the nature of military strategy and geopolitical relations and ushered in the nuclear age.

If the atomic bomb pushed the boundaries of engineering in unprecedented ways, so did the airplane that carried it. The Superfortress doubled the most critical performance measures of the B-17—payload and range—and featured innovations including a pressurized cabin, integral navigation and bombing radar, and a centralized fire-control computer. This dramatic leap in capability came at a heavy price in men and aircraft. American manufacturers struggled with the precision tolerances of the Superfortress

design, rushing it into service, while aircrews struggled with its complexity. Of the 3,763 B–29s accepted by the Army Air Forces during the war, only 1,544 made it overseas.

Despite having "more bugs than the Smithsonian entomology collection," as Gen. Curtis LeMay once quipped, the B–29 was at the apex of the American industrial war machine and the Army Air Forces never wavered in its belief that the B–29 was the key to victory in the Pacific.

In all, B–29s flew nearly 32,000 missions and dropped 170,000 tons of bombs as well as 9,300 aquatic mines that crippled internal movements in the Japanese empire. By war's end, 414 Superfortresses failed to return and 791 B–29 crewmen were killed or taken prisoner.

The *Enola Gay,* named for the mother of the 509th Composite Group's commander, Col. Paul Tibbets, was one of fifteen B–29s heavily modified for atomic delivery as part of the Silverplate program. It undertook its history-making mission stripped of nearly all armament and without escort. That such a mission was even possible was a testament to the previous operations of hundreds of other B–29 combat crews along with the thousands of marines, sailors, soldiers, and airmen who undertook the invasions of the islands required to launch such an assault.

ABOVE: SINCE 2003, THE *ENOLA GAY* HAS BEEN PROMINENTLY DISPLAYED AT THE UDVAR-HAZY CENTER.

LEFT: ON AUGUST 6, 1945, COL. PAUL TIBBETS OCCUPIED THIS SEAT AS AIRPLANE COMMANDER IN ADDITION TO COMMANDING THE 509TH COMPOSITE GROUP TASKED WITH THE ATOMIC MISSION. B-29 MANUALS EMPHASIZED THAT A SUPERFORTRESS AIRPLANE COMMANDER WAS "NO LONGER JUST A PILOT" AND WAS OVERSEEING "A COMBAT FORCE ALL YOUR OWN."

FORWARD CREW COMPARTMENT

1
COL. PAUL TIBBETS
Mission Commander

2
MAJ. THOMAS
FEREBEE
Bombardier

3
CAPT. ROBERT
LEWIS
Copilot

4
STAFF SGT. WYATT
DUZENBURY
Flight Engineer

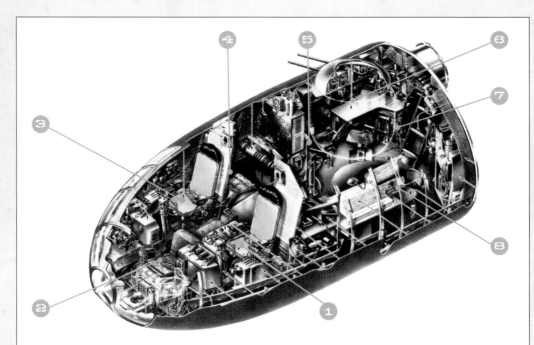

The forward crew compartment of the *Enola Gay* lacked the gun turret installations depicted here, but had Lt. Jeppson's atomic weapon monitoring equipment installed next to the radio operator's station.

5
2ND LT. MORRIS
JEPPSON
Bomb Electronics
Test Officer

6
CPL. RICHARD
NELSON
Radio Operator

7
CAPT. WILLIAM
PARSONS, USN
Bomb Commander

8
CAPT. THEODORE
"DUTCH" VAN KIRK
Navigator

NORMALLY, CAPT. ROBERT LEWIS FLEW AS THE AIRPLANE COMMANDER OF V-82 AS THIS B-29 WAS

DESIGNATED, BUT 509TH COMPOSITE GROUP COMMANDER PAUL TIBBETS TOOK OVER AS AIRPLANE

COMMANDER ON THE AUGUST 6 MISSION AND LEWIS ASSISTED AS COPILOT, DISPLACING THE CREW'S

NORMAL RIGHT-SEATER, LT. RICHARD MCNAMARA, FROM THE MISSION.

ABOVE: MANY AIRCRAFT INSTRUMENTS, SWITCHES, AND INSTRUCTION PLACARDS USED

PHOTOLUMINESCENT PAINT THAT WOULD GLOW IN THE PRESENCE OF A UV LIGHT. AND THESE

LIGHTS WERE PLACED LIBERALLY AROUND THE AIRCRAFT. A FEW CRITICAL CONTROLS

HAD MINUTE AMOUNTS OF RADIUM MIXED WITH THE PAINT, ENSURING THE ABILITY

TO SEE THEM IN THE EVENT OF A TOTAL ELECTRICAL FAILURE.

LEFT: STAFF SGT. WYATT DUZENBURY OCCUPIED THIS POSITION AS FLIGHT ENGINEER ON THE

ENOLA GAY WHERE HE STARTED AND MAINTAINED THE ENGINES AND OTHER CRITICAL SYSTEMS

ON THE AIRCRAFT. HIS REAR-FACING POSITION ALLOWED HIM TO MONITOR ALL FOUR OF THE

POTENTIALLY TROUBLESOME R-3350 ENGINES VISUALLY WITH ONLY A SMALL TWIST OF HIS HEAD.

ABOVE: THE RIGHT REAR OF THE COMPARTMENT CONTAINED THE RADIO OPERATOR'S
POSITION OCCUPIED BY CPL. RICHARD NELSON. IT ALSO HOUSED THE SP-1 (ATOMIC)
WEAPON MONITORING STATION OPERATED BY 2ND LT. MORRIS JEPPSON, WHO DIDN'T
HAVE THE LUXURY OF THE SEAT SEEN HERE (INSTALLED POST WAR).

RIGHT: CAPT. VAN KIRK DID NOT OPERATE THE RADAR, BUT HE WAS THE
ONLY MEMBER OF THE FORWARD CREW COMPARTMENT WHO COULD SEE THE AN/APQ-13
RADAR IMAGE. MOUNTED IN FRONT OF HIS CHARTING TABLE WAS AN AIR POSITION
INDICATOR—A SOPHISTICATED ELECTROMECHANICAL DEAD-RECKONING COMPUTER.

LOOKING BACK DOWN THE CREW TUNNEL FROM THE FORWARD CREW COMPARTMENT. THE DOME

WAS PRINCIPALLY FOR THE NAVIGATOR TO TAKE ASTRONOMICAL SIGHTINGS WITH

A SEXTANT, OR THE ASTROCOMPASS SEEN MOUNTED HERE. THE BOXLIKE STRUCTURE WAS

THE ATOMIC BOMB ACCESS PORT BUILT INTO THE TOP OF THE FORWARD BOMB BAY.

CREW TUNNEL LOOKING FORWARD. THE NEARLY 36-FOOT-LONG PADDED TUBE

CONNECTED THE FORWARD AND AFT PRESSURIZED CREW COMPARTMENTS. THE HATCH BELOW

THE TUNNEL PROVIDED ACCESS TO THE AFT BOMB BAY THAT INCLUDED THE SYSTEMS

FOR EMERGENCY GEAR AND BOMB BAY DOOR EXTENSION.

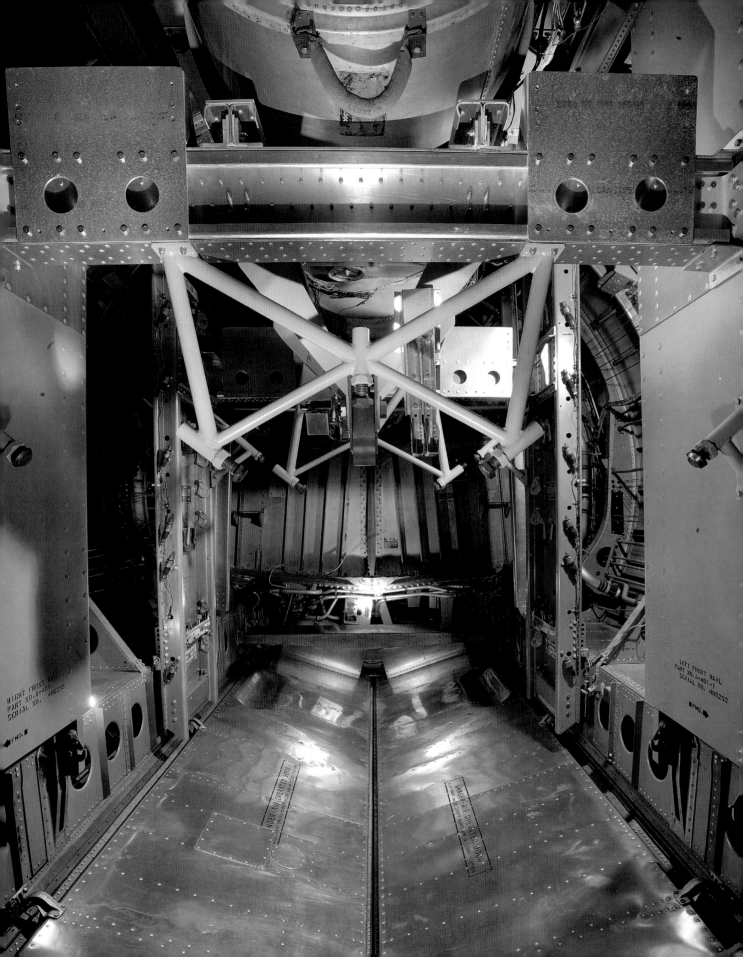

TOP: THE 8,900-LB *LITTLE BOY* HAD TO BE LOADED
INTO THE *ENOLA GAY* BY A LIFT BUILT INTO
A SPECIAL PIT ON TINIAN. THE BOMB ITSELF
CONTAINED A MERE 141 LBS OF URANIUM, BUT
EVEN THIS SMALL AMOUNT COST THE NATION OVER
A BILLION DOLLARS AND THE LABOR OF TENS OF
THOUSANDS OF PEOPLE, ONLY A HANDFUL OF WHOM
KNEW THE PURPOSE OF THEIR WORK.

MIDDLE: THESE ARMING PLUGS WERE FOUND
BEHIND THE RADIO OPERATOR'S POSITION DURING
RESTORATION OF THE AIRCRAFT. TO ARM THE *LITTLE
BOY* BOMB AFTER TAKEOFF, CAPT. WILLIAM PARSONS,
USN AND 2ND LT. MORRIS JEPPSON REMOVED THE
PRE-INSTALLED GREEN SAFING PLUGS AND INSERTED
THE RED ARMING PLUGS. THE GREEN PLUG IS LIKELY
FROM THE HIROSHIMA MISSION WHILE THE RED WAS
EITHER A SPARE OR FROM A TRAINING RUN.

BOTTOM: THE SP-1 UNIT USED TO MONITOR
THE ATOMIC BOMB CURRENTLY IN THE *ENOLA GAY*
IS A POSTWAR MODEL THAT WAS TO BE USED
DURING THE *CROSSROADS* TESTS AT BIKINI ATOLL
IN 1946. UNFORTUNATELY, THE ORIGINAL
MODEL SEEN HERE HAS NOT BEEN LOCATED.

LEFT: THIS IS THE VIEW CAPT. WILLIAM PARSONS,
USN AND 2ND LT. MORRIS JEPPSON HAD OF THE
FORWARD BOMB BAY FROM THE FORWARD CREW
COMPARTMENT. BOTH WOULD HAVE ENTERED THE BOMB
BAY THROUGH THIS HATCHWAY WITH THE AIRCRAFT
UNPRESSURIZED TO ARM THE ATOMIC BOMB.

THE GREEN ZINC CHROMATED COMPONENTS SEEN IN THE FORWARD BOMB BAY ARE THE SPECIAL

MODIFICATIONS USED TO ACCOMMODATE THE *LITTLE BOY* URANIUM AND *FAT MAN* PLUTONIUM

ATOMIC BOMBS. THE REAR BOMB BAY CONTAINED TWO AUXILIARY FUEL TANKS FOR THE MISSION.

THREE OPENINGS AT THE TOP PROVIDED ACCESS TO THE CREW TUNNEL. TWO WERE FOR

ELECTRICAL CONNECTORS FOR THE *LITTLE BOY* BOMB AND THE THIRD WAS A VIEWPORT.

AFT CREW COMPARTMENT

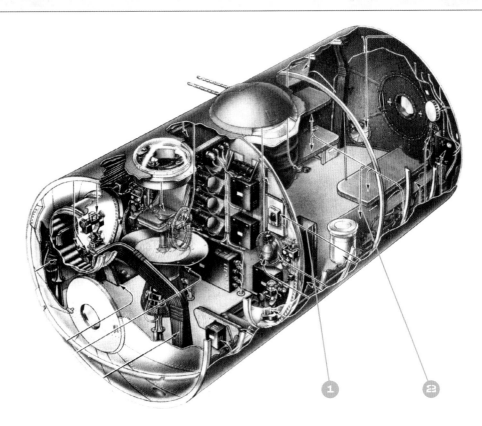

The aft crew compartment illustrated here depicts the crew bunks carried on some early B-29s, but which were replaced by the radar operator's station on the *Enola Gay* and many other Superfortresses. Also absent for Silverplate B-29s were the turrets, the gunners' dorsal and side-mounted sighting domes, and the complex (and heavy) central fire control system.

1
1ST LT. JACOB BESER
Radar
Countermeasures
Officer

2
STAFF SGT. JOSEPH
STIBORIK
Radar Operator

ABOVE: 1ST LT. JACOB BESER OCCUPIED THE RAVEN (RADAR COUNTERMEASURES) POSITION IN

THE REAR COMPARTMENT WHILE SITTING ON THE FLOOR WITHOUT A CHAIR. HE USED AN ARRAY

OF SURVEILLANCE RECEIVERS AND ANALYZERS TO DETERMINE ANY JAPANESE ELECTRONIC

RESPONSE TO THEIR APPROACH AND, IF NECESSARY, TO ALERT THE WEAPONEER TO ANY SIGNALS

THAT MIGHT PREMATURELY SET OFF THE RADAR FUSES ON THE ATOMIC BOMB AS IT FELL SIX

MILES TO ITS INTENDED DETONATION ALTITUDE OF 1,860 FEET.

LEFT: ON MOST B-29S, THE FORWARD PORTION OF THE AFT COMPARTMENT CONTAINED THE

GUNNERS' STATION WHERE THE TOP AND SIDE GUNNERS USED A CENTRALIZED

FIRE-CONTROL COMPUTER AND SIGHTING SYSTEMS TO ENGAGE ENEMY AIRCRAFT WITH TWO UPPER

AND TWO LOWER TURRETS. THESE WERE REMOVED, AS WERE THE SIGHTING BUBBLES ON

THE TOP AND SIDES OF THE COMPARTMENT, TO REDUCE WEIGHT AND DRAG, GIVING ADEQUATE

RANGE FOR THE ATOMIC MISSIONS.

STAFF SGT. JOSEPH STIBORIK OPERATED THE AN/APQ-13 NAVIGATION RADAR FROM

THIS POSITION. THE BLACK BOX BEHIND THE SCOPE IN IT IS AN AN/APQ-5

RADAR BOMBING ADAPTER THAT COUPLED THE RADAR TO THE NORDEN BOMBSIGHT.

TAIL SECTION

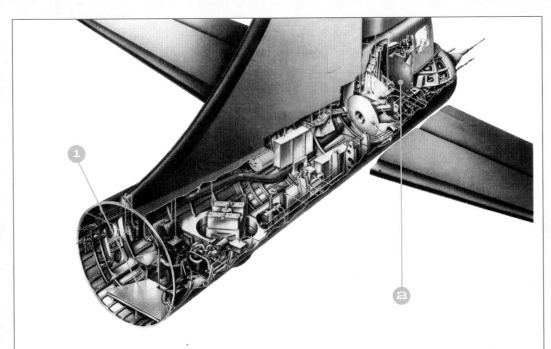

The *Enola Gay* carried only two .50 caliber machine guns for defensive armament and lacked the 20mm cannon depicted here.

1
SGT. ROBERT SHUMARD
Asst. Flight Enginner

2
SGT. GEORGE "BOB" CARON
Tail Gunner

THE SPACE AFT OF THE REAR CREW COMPARTMENT HOUSED A CAMERA BAY,

SOMETIMES ALSO USED FOR DISPENSING "ROPE," A FORM OF RADAR JAMMING CHAFF.

THE BLACK MOTOR IS THE "PUTT PUTT"--AN AUXILIARY POWER UNIT USED WHEN

STARTING THE AIRCRAFT. ASSISTANT FLIGHT ENGINEER SGT. ROBERT SHUMARD WOULD

HAVE MONITORED IT CLOSELY ON TAKEOFF AND LANDING.

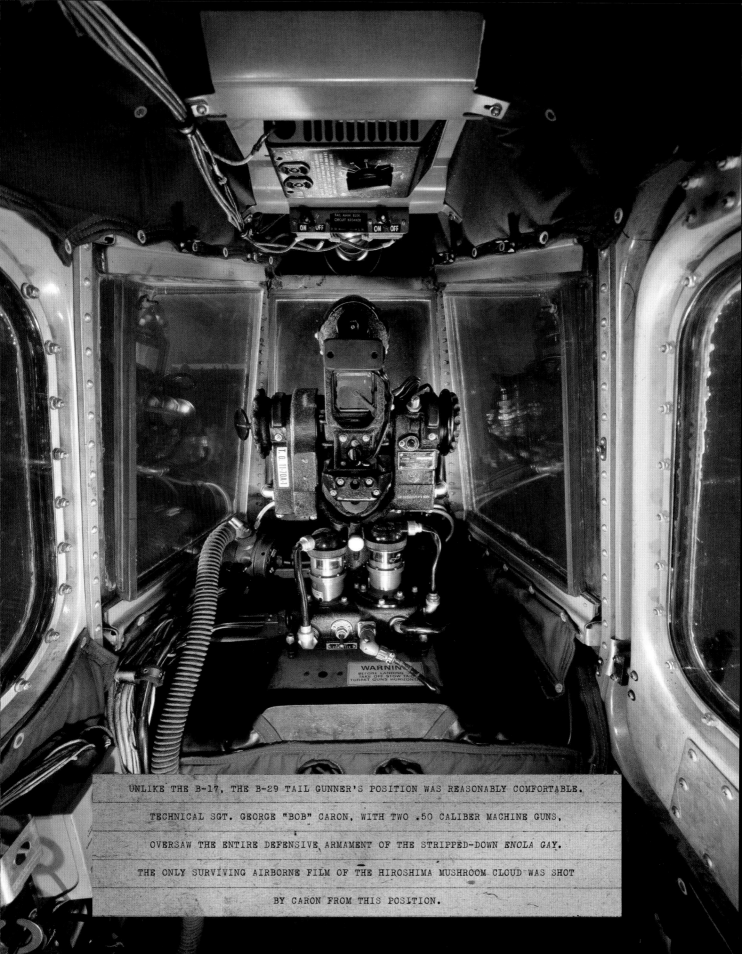

UNLIKE THE B-17, THE B-29 TAIL GUNNER'S POSITION WAS REASONABLY COMFORTABLE.

TECHNICAL SGT. GEORGE "BOB" CARON, WITH TWO .50 CALIBER MACHINE GUNS,

OVERSAW THE ENTIRE DEFENSIVE ARMAMENT OF THE STRIPPED-DOWN *ENOLA GAY*.

THE ONLY SURVIVING AIRBORNE FILM OF THE HIROSHIMA MUSHROOM CLOUD WAS SHOT

BY CARON FROM THIS POSITION.

BOEING (STEARMAN) N2S-5 KAYDET

The Boeing (Stearman) Kaydet primary trainer is one of the iconic aircraft of the 1930s and 1940s. An entire generation of pilots who learned to fly in the Kaydet went on to fight in the hostile skies of World War II. The Kaydet was produced in greater numbers than almost any other military biplane. After its days as the backbone of the Army and Navy primary training program, it began a second career as a crop duster. Today, it remains one of the most beloved vintage aircraft still flying.

Lloyd Carlton Stearman was a talented airplane designer who started his own company in 1926. Three years later, the company became part of the United Aircraft and Transport conglomerate, which owned several companies, including Boeing. In 1934, a government trust-busting suit broke up the company and Stearman ended up as a subsidiary of Boeing. Keeping its identity at first, the company eventually ended up as the Wichita Division of Boeing in 1941. Despite the legalities, the beloved Kaydet continues to be called a "Stearman" to this day.

In the early 1930s, with the Depression hitting hard, Stearman sought military contracts to stay afloat. First orders came from the Navy for the company's Model 73 (Navy designation NS–1) with a Wright J–5 engine. An improved model with a Lycoming R–680 engine was adopted by the Army in 1935 and became the PT–13. Nicknamed the Kaydet, production continued for 10 years until war's end in 1945. Approximately 8,500 were produced.

In 1940, the Navy ordered its first Kaydets and designated them N2S–2 and –5. Models with alternate engines were designated as Army PT–17, PT–18, and Navy N2S–1, –3 and –4. The only complete standardization of any U.S. Army and Navy aircraft during the war was the Boeing-Stearman PT–13D/N2S–5. This N2S–5 was built in December 1943 and trained naval pilots at the Naval Air Station in Ottumwa, Iowa, until 1946.

Being a primary trainer, the cockpit of the N2S–5 was a simple affair. On the left, from back to front, are the elevator trim handle and the throttle and mixture controls. The red lever just in front of the rudder pedal locked the controls when the aircraft was parked. A red fuel shutoff switch is located under the panel on the left and the parking brake lever is on the right. Mounted to the right of the cockpit is the fire extinguisher with the instrument light rheostat switch just behind it.

N2S-5 ON DISPLAY AT THE UDVAR-HAZY CENTER.

A NAVAL RATING WINDS THE INERTIAL STARTER.

CURTISS SB2C-5 HELLDIVER

The Helldiver began in 1938 as a carrier-based dive-bomber replacement for the Douglas SBD Dauntless. For many pilots, the Helldiver (commonly known as "The Beast") was a troublesome substitute for the venerable Dauntless despite a successful campaign record. Though the SB2C was more capable than the SBD in nearly every performance measure, pilots often judged it more difficult to handle and innovations, such as an electrically controllable propeller and a complex hydraulic system, proved problematic. Later-model Helldivers were more reliable and ended the war with an improved reputation.

The Helldiver was slow to enter service due to a number of production delays. Though more than 5,500 were constructed, the first combat use of the aircraft did not occur until November 1943 during an attack on Rabaul. Navy Helldivers experienced intense combat in the Mariana Islands and in the Battle of Leyte Gulf, where they played a decisive role in the final devastation of the Japanese carrier force. One pilot in that operation who aided in the destruction of the Japanese carrier Zuikaku (a participant in the attack on Pearl Harbor) was a young lieutenant (jg) named Donald Engen, who later became the director of the National Air and Space Museum.

This example is a late-production SB2C-5 that did not see combat service, but it is remarkable as one of only a handful of surviving Helldivers. It was photographed while in storage and the canopy structures were not installed.

One of the features that made the SB2C-5 such an improvement over its predecessors was a much-enhanced cockpit layout. The panel was unusual in having an overlay that at first appears to be misplaced. It seems to partially cover up some crucial instruments, such as the artificial horizon, but the dive indicator above and to the right of the horizon provided adequate vertical guidance in descents. The oscilloscope to the left of the horizon is for the AN/APS-4 surface search radar. The red knob on the far left side of the front panel operated the wing-folding mechanism for carrier stowage. The large wheel on the right side opened and closed the canopy.

The rear gunner/radar operator sat in a swivel seat with twin .30 caliber machine guns on a flexible ring mount. The upper rear fuselage in front of the vertical stabilizer is a collapsible "turtleback" that gave the guns freedom of movement to the rear.

THROTTLE QUADRANT ON LEFT SIDE OF THE PILOT'S COCKPIT.

RADAR OPERATOR/GUNNER'S POSITION.

CURTISS-WRIGHT XP-55 ASCENDER

The outbreak of war in Europe forced the Air Corps to reconsider the conservative approach to aircraft design that it had maintained during the 1930s. Manufacturers, such as Curtiss-Wright, gained development contracts for unconventional designs, like the pusher fighter proposal that became the XP-55. The Ascender, with its double entendre name, was one of three USAAF "pusher" fighter prototypes that ultimately proved to have too many novel features to compete successfully with the more conventional wartime models.

Curtiss-Wright began development in June 1940 and by July 1943, had completed the first of three XP-55 airframes built around the Allison V-1710-95 liquid-cooled engine. One advantage of the pusher/canard configuration was that it allowed for the installation of four .50 caliber machine guns in the nose without concern for the convergence issues of wing-mounted guns.

Unfortunately, the Ascender suffered from shortcomings in performance, particularly its unpredictable stall response. Other issues, such as a marginal roll rate and poor rearward visibility combined to discourage Army Air Forces interest in future production. The XP-55's pusher peers, the Vultee XP-54 Swoose Goose, and Northrop XP-56 Black Bullet, fared no better.

As a prototype demonstrator, the XP-55 lacked many refinements standard on production combat aircraft, and without blind flying instruments it was only suited to daylight testing in good visibility. An unusual feature was an automatic engine control akin to that employed on the Focke-Wulf Fw 190. The throttle coordinated rpm and manifold pressure together, though a "modifier control" on the right side of the throttle quadrant allowed increased boosting of the manifold pressure beyond standard. Unlike the Fw 190, the mixture control operated in the conventional manner.

The pusher propeller made bailout more complicated and the pilot had to remember to close the throttle and mixture, open the cowl flaps, and then pull the propeller jettison control (bottom red handle on the right). This shifted the center of gravity of the plane forward and while the pilot dealt with this condition, he had to pull the canopy jettison handle (located just above the propeller jettison handle). One pilot did make a successful bailout, but only after losing 16,000 feet (another was not so lucky). This example is the only one of the three XP-55 prototypes that survived the war.

THE XP-55 ON LOAN TO THE KALAMAZOO AIR ZOO.

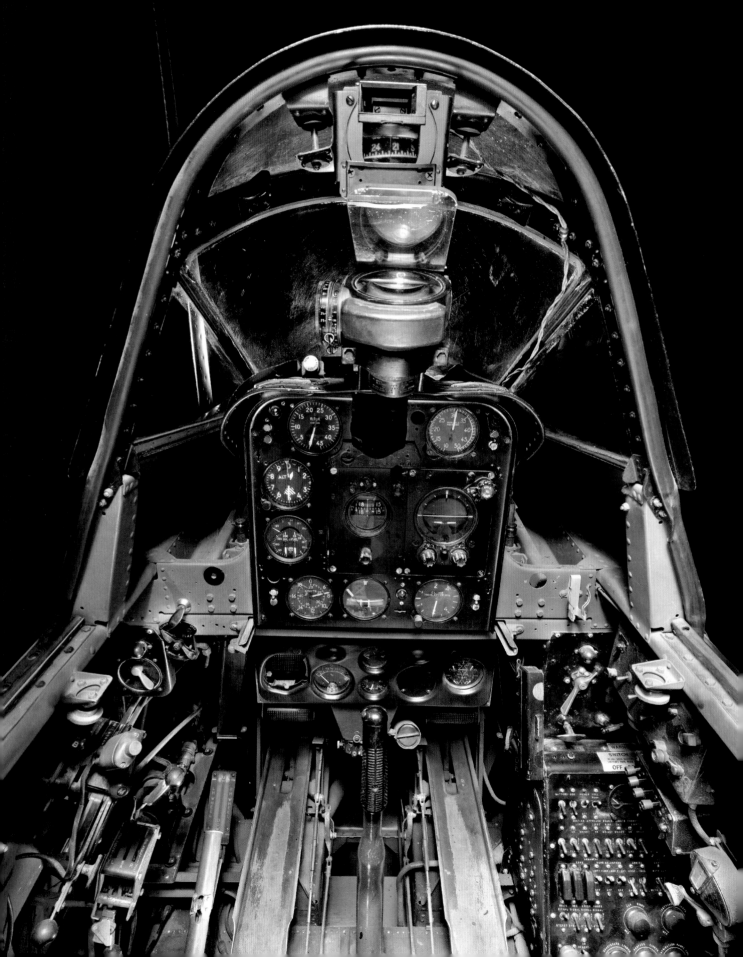

DOUGLAS SBD-6 DAUNTLESS

Nearing obsolescence at the start of World War II, the Douglas SBD Dauntless served throughout the entire conflict, becoming one of the most important naval aircraft in the Pacific Theater. The so-called Slow But Deadly (a play on SBD) was the primary fleet shipboard bomber in the early phase of the war when the only means of striking back against Japanese forces was with carrier-launched aircraft. In 1942, SBDs sank more enemy shipping than any other aircraft. At the Battles of the Coral Sea and Midway, SBDs destroyed almost half of the enemy aircraft carrier force, effectively stopping Japanese expansion and turning the tide of the war in the Pacific.

In 1934, the U.S. Navy's Bureau of Aeronautics (BuAer) initiated planning to replace its fabric-covered biplanes with modern all-metal aircraft. Northrop Corporation submitted the winning design in the single engine bomber category. Shortly thereafter, Douglas Aircraft, the majority shareholder in Northrop, bought out the company and dissolved it. As a result, the new aircraft was accepted as the SBD (Scout Bomber Douglas) and named the Dauntless.

The first production model, the SBD–1, was found unsuitable for shipboard operations because of limited range and the Marine Corps employed them in land-based operations. After improvements and fleet acceptance, the SBD underwent near-continuous modification in an attempt to increase combat capability and performance, including installation of more powerful engines, and surface search radar in later models.

The SBD–6 was the final version and this example is the sixth of this model built. The U.S. Army Air Corps, awed by the performance of German Stukas, but not having dive-bombers of their own, bought the SBD and called it the A–24 Banshee. Despite their early combat success, the Dauntless slowly ceded the naval dive-bombing mission to the long-delayed Curtiss SB2C Helldiver. Abandoned in 1944 by the Navy, the venerable SBD would finish the war—where it started—with the Marine Corps.

The right side of the cockpit mounts the controls for the landing gear and flaps. Selecting "Diving Flap" and operating the engine hydraulic pump control at the rear of the panel extended the upper and lower portions of the split flaps. The dive flaps could be opened at any speed and slowed the aircraft to allow for more accurate bombing. The gaps on the left and right sides of the instrument panel were mounts for the .30 caliber machine guns (now missing). The reflector gunsight at center top of the control panel was introduced on the SBD–5 and replaced the obsolete telescopic site found on earlier models.

THE GUNNER ALSO OPERATED THE SBD'S RADIO GEAR.

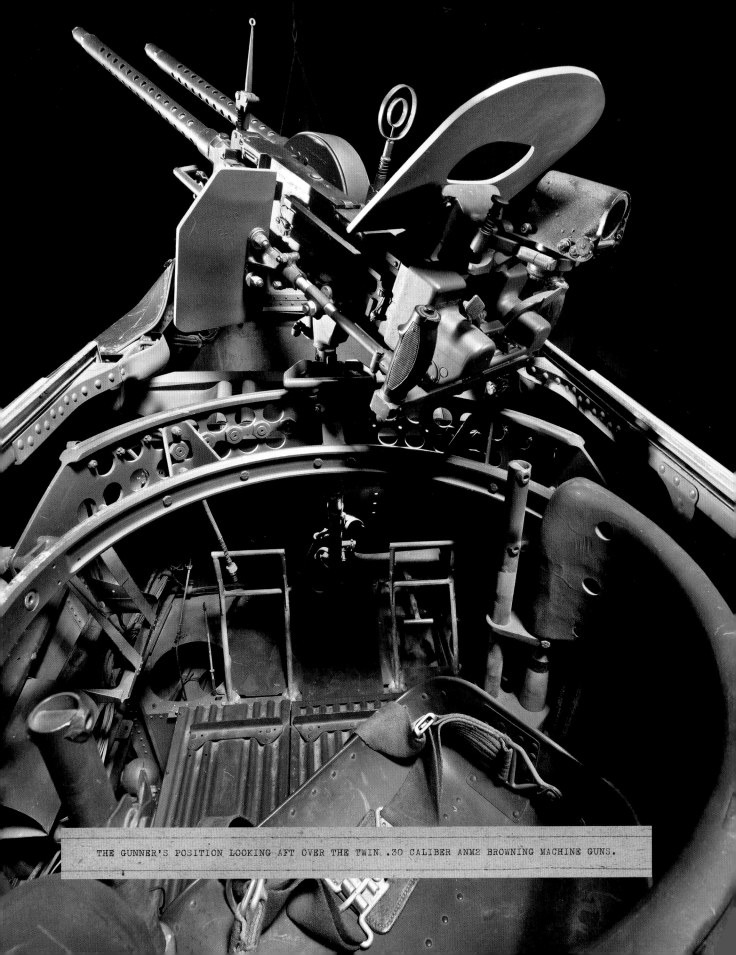

THE GUNNER'S POSITION LOOKING AFT OVER THE TWIN .30 CALIBER ANM2 BROWNING MACHINE GUNS.

EASTERN AIRCRAFT FM-1 (GRUMMAN F4F-4) WILDCAT

In the mid–1930s, the U.S. Navy was looking to replace its biplane fighters with modern, all-metal monoplanes. The Navy asked Grumman to submit a design as a backup to the Brewster F2A Buffalo. Due to the Buffalo's poor performance, the resulting Grumman F4F Wildcat became the Navy and Marine Corps' primary fighter aircraft in the early years of the war. Produced in some 20 variants, the Wildcat was the only naval fighter to serve operationally from the beginning to the end of the war.

The first production Wildcat, the F4F–3, entered service in December 1940. Early combat experience revealed that the Wildcat was inferior in performance to the Japanese Zero. Wildcat pilots, however, soon learned to use their aircraft's strengths, along with new tactics, to hold their own against the Japanese fighter.

In late 1941, the F4F–4 model was introduced. This variant had folding wings for more efficient carrier operations and increased the armament from four .50 caliber machine guns to six. By 1943, Grumman was concentrating on the new F6F Hellcat, but the Navy still needed Wildcats. General Motors's Eastern Aircraft Division therefore took over production of the Wildcat and produced more of them than Grumman. Designated FM–1s, the new Wildcats were essentially the same as the F4F–4 model with the exception of a return to four machine guns. The final version of the Wildcat was the FM-2. With a lightened airframe and more powerful engine it was the ideal fighter for the escort carriers and was produced in higher quantities than any other Wildcat model.

Two features of the Wildcat cockpit immediately define it as a naval fighter. Prominent on the left side rail of the cockpit is a black and yellow handle. This was the control for the tail hook used for landing on aircraft carriers. The second feature is the chart table found on many single-seat naval aircraft. Operating over water, where landmarks were nonexistent, naval aviators had to be proficient in navigation. Another unusual feature for a modern fighter was the hand crank used to raise and lower the landing gear. Just visible on the right side, it is below the electrical panel. Raising the landing gear inevitably introduced a roller-coaster effect as the pilot's body transferred the motion of each turn of the crank to the control stick.

ABOVE: LEND-LEASE MARTLET VARIANT BOUND FOR GREAT BRITAIN PRIOR TO SHIPMENT.

RIGHT: THE EXTENDABLE NAVIGATION TABLE WAS ESSENTIAL FOR PLOTTING POSITIONS

RELATIVE TO THE WILDCAT'S CONSTANTLY MOVING BATTLE GROUP.

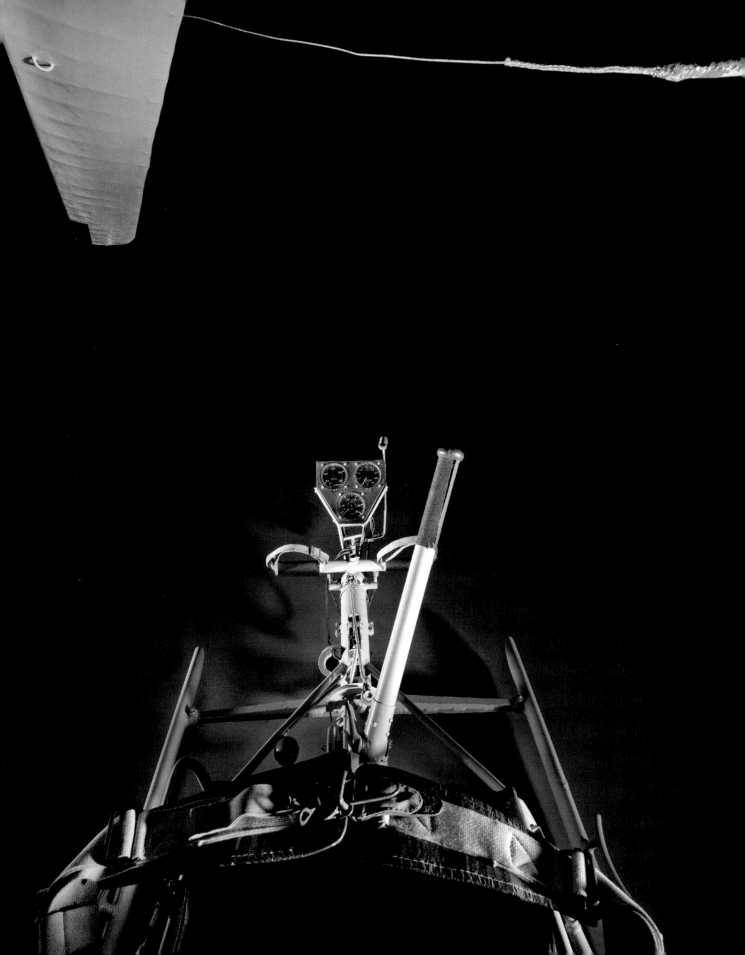

FOCKE ACHGELIS
FA 330 A-1 BACHSTELZE

The Fa 330 rotary wing kite was an ingenious (if not entirely practical) solution to a requirement for increasing the spotting range of U-boats. Stored in two vertical tubes in the U-boat's conning tower, the Fa 330 could be assembled and disassembled in about three minutes without special tools using a series of quick-release pins (painted yellow). Several more minutes were required to tow the aircraft aloft or retrieve it.

The Bachstelze (Water Wagtail) also had to be simple to fly so that minimally trained enlisted personnel could operate it. Candidates received basic glider training and then moved on to the gyro kite. Fa 330 training occurred in a French wind tunnel, or by being towed behind trucks on the Autobahn, and then at sea towed by E-boats (German torpedo boats). The kite was pulled aloft in autorotation by the U-boat at a relative wind speed of around 35 kilometers per hour, which usually meant that the U-boat would have to move directly into the wind. On windy days, the 300-meter towrope that doubled as the communications cable, allowed the Fa 330 to reach a maximum altitude of 220 meters, giving a potential sighting distance of 35 kilometers.

The Bachstelze featured a remarkable escape system. If the U-boat came under attack and had to crash dive, the pilot pulled the red quick-release lever below the rotor head labeled *"Auslösung"* (release), dropping the towline, separating the rotor hub from the mast, and deploying a parachute as the airframe and pilot fell away. The pilot then released his seat buckle, allowing the remainder of the structure to drop. The abandoned pilot would bob about in the ocean until the attack was over and the U-boat could surface and recover the crew member. For noncombat emergencies, the towline quick-release coupling was operated by pulling the red handle to the left of the control stick. There are no accounts of this system actually being employed.

Around 200 Fa 330s were built and were ready for operational deployment in early 1943, but the Battle of the Atlantic was almost over and for a U-boat to deploy one in the heavily patrolled Atlantic would have been suicidal. They did serve in the Indian Ocean and one spotted a merchant vessel that its U-boat subsequently torpedoed, but there are no other surviving records of successful employments. Deploying a Bachstelze put the U-boat at great risk for visual or radar detection and constrained the submarine's maneuverability and the concept must be regarded as a failure.

THE FA 330 ROTOR HEAD FEATURED COLOR-CODED MARKINGS TO ENSURE THAT
THE BALANCED BLADE SET ATTACHED TO THE CORRECT POINTS. THE YELLOW FITTINGS
ARE QUICK-RELEASE PINS FOR RAPID ASSEMBLY.

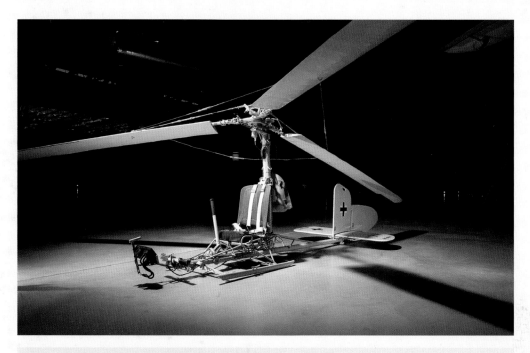

TOP: FA 330 ON DISPLAY AT THE UDVAR-HAZY CENTER.

BOTTOM: A U-BOAT PREPARING TO LAUNCH AN FA 330.

FOCKE-WULF FW 190 D-9

In 1942, the Luftwaffe issued a requirement for a new high-altitude fighter to counter expected American bomber formations operating above 24,000 feet. Focke-Wulf began designing what would eventually become the excellent Ta 152 fighter. Progress was so slow, however, that in July of 1943 a stopgap aircraft was ordered.

Focke-Wulf complied by adding the Junkers Jumo 213A in-line water-cooled engine, which had previously been used only in bombers, to an Fw 190 A–8 airframe. The nose was strengthened and lengthened to accommodate the engine, as was the rear fuselage. Armament consisted of two 20 mm cannons in the wings and two 13 mm machine guns above the engine. The Jumo 213A's increased reliability and performance made the new Fw 190 D-9 superior to the previous models in climb, dive, and level speed.

Introduced in the summer of 1944, the first production model was designated the Fw 190 D–9 and was nicknamed the "Dora 9." Also known as the *Langnasen* (Long Nose) for its stretched cowling, the new model would become popular with its pilots despite initial reluctance to what was viewed as a "bomber" engine. The Fw 190 D–9 was found to be more than a match for frontline fighters in several critical performance areas, such as speed and acceleration. As with the rest of the Luftwaffe, however, fuel shortages in the closing months of the war would restrict its use.

For pilots used to the cramped confines of the Messerschmitt Me 109, the Focke-Wulf was relatively roomy. The bubble canopy also offered better visibility.

Painted a dark gray to reduce glare, the cockpit of the Dora 9 is very similar to other Fw 190 models and features the *Kommandogerät* mechanical "brain" that coordinated the operation of the throttle, mixture, and propeller pitch through the use of a single power lever. Combined with automated supercharger and oil-cooler controls, this system greatly reduced the workload on pilots in high-altitude maneuvering dogfights. At the front of the right side panel is an empty space that would have contained a clock—a highly popular item to be taken as a souvenir from aircraft and, thus, missing on many panels today. The red dots on the instruments are not original and indicate that they have been checked for radiation. The Revi gunsight is not present, but would be located at the top of the instrument panel, just right of center. The windscreen rear frame was not present when the aircraft was received, and so a wooden piece has been mocked up for display.

FW 190 D-9 ON DISPLAY AT THE NATIONAL MUSEUM OF THE U.S. AIR FORCE.

FOCKE-WULF FW 190 F-8

Diving out of the sun over Dunkirk, France, and shooting down three Spitfire Mk Vs with no losses to themselves, four Focke-Wulf Fw 190s made the type's combat debut in September 1941. The Allies were taken by surprise by the previously unknown fighter. Designed from 1937 to 1939 as a backup to the Messerschmitt Me 109, the *Würger* (Shrike), as it was known in the field, would go on to perform in several roles and become one of the outstanding fighter aircraft of the war.

The Fw 190 was designed around an air-cooled radial engine and, in fact, was the only operational German fighter to have that type of power plant. The design included a bubble canopy, which gave the pilot excellent visibility, and a widely spaced landing gear that provided stability and allowed the aircraft to operate from primitive airfields. Beginning life as an air superiority fighter, the Fw 190 evolved through numerous variants and subvariants, with a bewildering variety of factory and field modification kits provided to perform a multitude of roles.

By 1942, the Luftwaffe decided that since earlier versions had performed well in the close ground-support role, a variant specifically designed for this was needed. The *Jabo* (short for *Jagdbomber* or fighter-bomber) version would be designated the Fw 190 F. With attachment points for bombs and increased armor under the engine and fuselage, the *Jabos* were excellent fighter-bombers, but paid a price in performance due to the extra weight.

This example is an Fw 190 F–8/R1, which entered service in 1944. It was identical to the Fw 190 A–8 fighter—the most-produced version of the Fw 190—with the addition of a central bomb rack and the removal of the outboard cannon to save weight. This variant could also be fitted with additional wing-mounted bomb racks, underwing 30 mm cannon, rockets, and various other modifications. This aircraft was originally built as an Fw 190 A–7 fighter, but was converted to an Fw 190 F–8 after suffering damage during operations. This example served with ground-attack wing SG2 in Hungary during the last months of the war.

The Fw 190 cockpit has an unusual segmented instrument panel. On top were the ammunition counters, the gunsight, and the radio navigation homing indicator. The separate main panel contained the flight and navigation instruments. Engine instruments were housed on a small panel below and recessed slightly from the main panel. The cockpit features the *Kommandogerät* power level discussed previously in regard to the Fw 190 D–9.

FW 190 F-8 ON DISPLAY AT THE UDVAR-HAZY CENTER.

OFTEN OVERLOOKED IN THE WEST, THE IL-2 WAS ARGUABLY THE MOST INFLUENTIAL TACTICAL COMBAT AIRCRAFT OF THE WAR.

ILYUSHIN IL-2 SHTURMOVIK

The Il-2 Shturmovik lingers in historical memory as the signature aircraft of the VVS (Soviet Air Force) in World War II. During the air war over the Russian front, the Soviets placed a key emphasis on tactical air operations. In what they called Combined Arms Warfare, all air units were mobilized to support the ground forces. Unlike the Anglo-American air forces, the Soviets did not develop a strategic air arm using long-range bombers. The Il-2 Shturmovik played a crucial, often devastating, role at the cutting edge of all Soviet offensives in World War II. With an estimated 36,000 built, it was the most-produced combat aircraft in history.

Sergei V. Ilyushin designed his so-called Winged Tank specifically for the requirements of the ground-attack mission. The Il-2 was constructed around a central armored steel shell, which offered protection to the engine, the fuel and oil tanks, and the pilot. It was armed with two 7.62 mm machine guns and two 20 mm (later 23 mm) cannons in the wings, which made it highly effective in attacks on enemy armor and mechanized units. The Germans feared it as the *Schwarzer Tod* (*black death*). To the Soviets, it was simply the Shturmovik (a generic term referring to any ground-attack aircraft).

Entering service as a single-seater, the Il-2 eventually was fitted with a rear gunner in the aftermath of high losses in air combat. The absence of armored protection in the rear, however, resulted in a high toll of losses for those airmen assigned as rear gunners. The Shturmovik would receive additional modifications to the wing to correct stability problems and upgrade armament. The IL–2 in the National Air and Space Museum collection received underwing 37 mm cannons to replace the wing-mounted ones.

This Il–2 is a rare aircraft, one of the few surviving examples of its type despite the large numbers produced. It was recovered from a lake near St. Petersburg (Leningrad) in the early 1990s and partially restored before being donated to the Smithsonian in 1995.

Cockpits in World War II Soviet aircraft were routinely austere with minimal attention to pilot comfort. On the control stick, the two buttons in the center are for the machine guns and cannons, while the bomb release and rocket buttons are on the left and right respectively. Originally fitted with a gunsight, later production Shturmoviks had a simplified sight of three aiming circles on the diamond-shaped area of the front windscreen. As World War II progressed, most Soviet frontline aircraft, including the Il–2, were equipped with radios.

ABOVE: IN 1944, THE NATIONAL AIR AND SPACE MUSEUM'S IL-2 WAS SHOT DOWN AND MADE A FORCED LANDING ON A FROZEN LAKE NEAR LENINGRAD (ST. PETERSBURG). OVER FOUR DECADES LATER, IT WAS PULLED FROM THE MUCK AND RESTORED.

RIGHT: THE GUNNER'S POSITION WITH A 12.7 MM BEREZIN UBT MACHINE GUN CAPABLE OF 38 DEGREES OF TRAVEL VERTICALLY AND 44 DEGREES HORIZONTALLY.

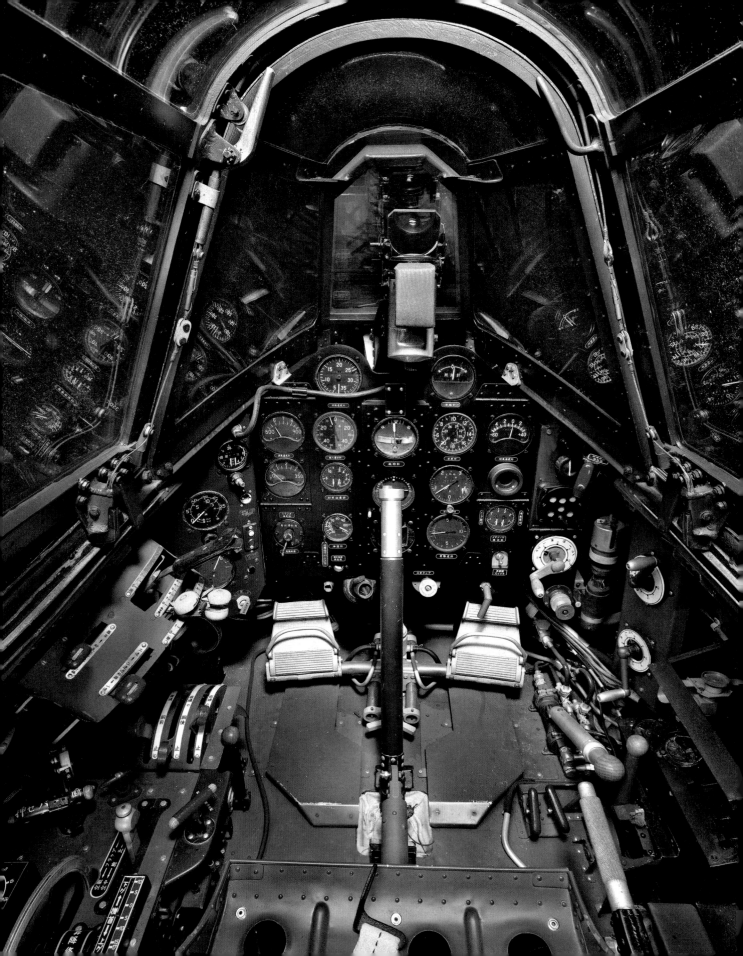

KAWANISHI N1K2-JA SHIDEN KAI "GEORGE"

The unlikely offspring of a Japanese floatplane fighter, the Kawanishi N1K2-Ja Shiden Kai, Allied codename "George," was built as a private venture. Initially spurned by the Japanese navy for its unofficial status, the Shiden (Violet Lightning) eventually became the best Japanese naval fighter of World War II.

In 1942, Kawanishi flew the prototype of a new floatplane fighter aircraft that, despite the handicap of large central and wingtip floats, proved to be almost as maneuverable and fast as the excellent Mitsubishi Zero. At the same time as the floatplane model was being developed, engineers at Kawanishi began work on a land-based version without government approval.

The new fighter differed little from its floatplane progenitor. A new, more powerful engine necessitated a long, ungainly landing gear to ensure that the nose was elevated enough for the large propeller to clear the ground. Another improvement was the addition of flaps that automatically deployed to reduce the chance of a stall during demanding combat maneuvers. This new, modified aircraft was designated the N1K1-J Shiden. Unfortunately, the engine was unreliable and the landing gear was weak. By 1943, however, the Japanese needed a fighter to counter the American Hellcats and Corsairs. Therefore, despite its shortcomings, the once-reluctant Japanese navy accepted the new Shiden fighter.

As the N1K1 entered production, engineers worked to correct its flaws. No alternative engine was available, but to correct the landing gear, the wing was lowered from its original midfuselage position, allowing installation of a normal length landing gear strut. A longer fuselage and redesigned tail improved

stability problems. The new aircraft was designated the N1K2-J Shiden Kai (modified).

The Shiden Kai soon proved to be a worthy opponent of the newer American fighters. Its use as a B-29 interceptor, however, was less successful due to poor high-altitude performance. Several variants were produced, such as this N1K2-Ja fighter-bomber model. Despite being an excellent fighter, the Shiden Kai appeared too late and in too small a quantity to affect the outcome of the war.

The instrument panel of the Shiden Kai was laid out with flying and engine instruments on the main panel. Oxygen and fuel gauges are on the left panel. One feature that stood out in Japanese aircraft is the use of wood in cockpit controls. Such usage of wood, especially late in the war when raw materials were scarce, served to illustrate the desperate condition of Japanese aircraft manufacturers. The tops of several levers, the trim wheel and the throttle handle, with its distinctive notched thumb rest, were all constructed of wood.

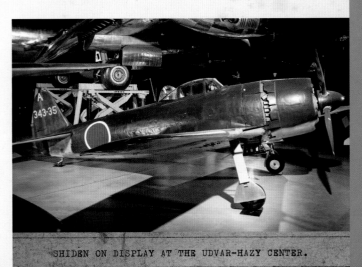

SHIDEN ON DISPLAY AT THE UDVAR-HAZY CENTER.

KELLETT XO-60

Nearly all of the major combatants during World War II experimented with autogiros during the 1930s for liaison and artillery observation, but they would come to play a minimal role in actual combat and those in the United States saw no operational use whatsoever. This class of aircraft had a freewheeling unpowered rotor that depended on continuous movement of air through it to generate lift. Autogiros had several desirable traits: They could land almost vertically, take off in shorter distances than fixed-wing planes, and fly slowly, giving a stable observation platform that was far more mobile than the tethered kite balloons of World War I. Demonstrations even showed they could climb to 2,000 feet while continuously connected to a telephone cable.

There was also much not to like. They were expensive, usually costing at least three times that of a comparably sized airplane, while having half the payload and slower cruise speeds. They could be easily damaged and if not handled very carefully while rolling on the ground, a condition known as ground resonance could result, which could cause catastrophic failure of the rotor system. By 1938, the U.S. Army Air Corps had decided to move away from autogiro development and toward STOL (Short Take-Off and Landing) planes along the lines of the Fieseler

Storch. In spite of this, Congress insisted on pushing an appropriation for a new generation of "jump giros" that could make true vertical takeoffs by overspeeding the rotor on the ground and engaging a mechanism that increased blade pitch for lift while simultaneously declutching the rotor and giving all power to the tractor propeller. This system avoided the torque problem of helicopters, so that no tail rotor was required, but these machines could not hover.

In the cockpit, the rotor mast dominated the pilot's field of vision. The control stick tilted the rotor hub for control (there was no cyclic pitch mechanism as on most helicopters), though the rudder was controlled as on any airplane. The large spring visible in the center of the cockpit is an adjustable rudder lock. The observer's cockpit had outstanding visibility in every direction except forward. A Plexiglas floor allowed for unrestricted downward sighting and a convenient map table facilitated artillery direction.

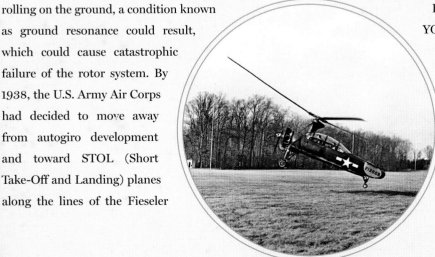

Kellett Aircraft built seven of the X/YO–60 jump giros, but by the time they were flying in 1943, Sikorsky's helicopters were outperforming them in nearly every measure with the added benefit of being able to hover. Thus, the O–60s, the last true autogiros built in the United States, were quietly withdrawn from testing.

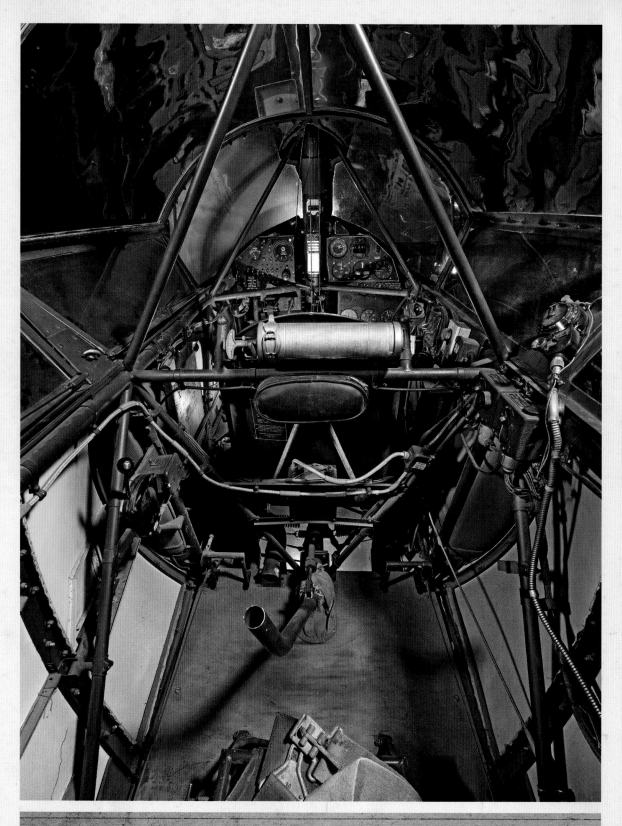

OBSERVER'S AUXILIARY PILOT POSITION.

OBSERVER'S PLOTTING TABLE LOOKING TO THE REAR.

KUGISHO MXY7 OHKA MODEL 22

As the Allied forces closed in on the Japanese home islands in 1944, the military leadership became desperate for a way to stop them. Vice Adm. Onishi Takijino recommended that the Imperial Japanese Navy form special units to conduct suicide attacks on American ships. Designated as *Tokko* (special attack) units, they would become known to the Allies as the "kamikaze."

The Tokko pilots flew almost every type of Japanese military aircraft, but their high loss rate revealed the need for an aircraft designed specifically for the one-way attack mission. Ensign Mitsuo Ohta envisioned a small, rocket-powered Tokko aircraft carried into battle by a long-range bomber. The First Naval Air Technical Bureau built it as the MXY7 Ohka (Cherry Blossom) Model 11.

The short duration burn of the Ohka's rocket engine resulted in a range of only 23 miles; thus it could not be released from its launching aircraft before coming into range of radar-directed U.S. Navy fighters. The disastrous combat debut of the Ohka saw the entire group of 16 G4M2 "Betty" mother ships shot down before reaching their launch point. The Ohka eventually did score several minor successes, including damaging the battleship *West Virginia*. Some were even used as manned air-to-air missiles against B–29 raids, but no successes in this role have been substantiated.

Kugisho attempted to solve the range problem by installing a hybrid power plant with an internal combustion engine driving a turbine. An auxiliary burner at the tail operated like an afterburner to increase thrust. The engine was started while still on the ground—saving the weight of an onboard starter—and it idled during the flight using fuel from the host aircraft. When the aircraft were within range, the turbine engine was spooled up and the fuel at the tail was ignited as the Ohka dropped away. By war's end, Kugisho had built 50 Ohka 22 airframes, though only three engines were completed and just one (unsuccessful) test flight was made. This Ohka 22 is the only surviving example of this hybrid power plant Tokko aircraft.

Befitting its expendable status, and its use by novice pilots, the cockpit of the Ohka 22 is simple. Basic flight instruments were located on the panel, with a crude rudder bar on the cockpit floor. The wooden throttle on the left wall controlled both fuel to the internal combustion engine and to the auxiliary burner at the tail. On the right, the red handle below the inclinometer armed the warhead located in the nose.

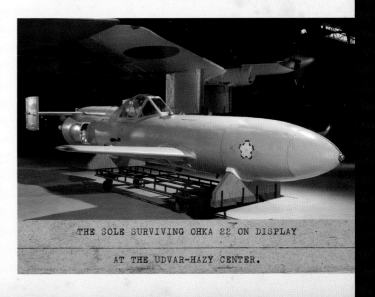

THE SOLE SURVIVING OHKA 22 ON DISPLAY AT THE UDVAR-HAZY CENTER.

KYUSHU J7W1 SHINDEN

Air combat during World War II pushed aircraft development in new directions. Both Allied and Axis countries tried to develop aircraft that would provide performance advantages over the enemy's designs. The Kyushu J7W1 Shinden (Magnificent Lightning) was one such aircraft. Its rear engine configuration and unusual shape made it one of the most distinctive aircraft of the war.

The J7W1 Shinden was the brainchild of Capt. Masaoko Tsuruno of the technical staff of the Imperial Japanese Navy. Encouraging glider test results prompted the Japanese navy to assign the prototype project to the Kyushu Hikoki K. K. firm—chosen for its availability to take on new work, not for its advanced design expertise. Because of this, additional engineers, including Tsuruno, were assigned to complete the project.

The Shinden was conceived as a jet-powered aircraft. However, a piston engine driving a six-bladed propeller was initially installed. The large rear-mounted propeller required an unusually long tricycle landing gear. Swept-back wings, vertical fins mounted inboard of the ailerons, and a canard highlighted its futuristic appearance. A powerful armament package of four 30 mm cannons mounted in the nose offset the heavy rear-mounted engine.

Work began on the J7W1 in June of 1944. Japan's precarious military situation forced the navy to order the Shinden into production even before the prototype was finished. Due to delays, the first prototype did not fly until just 12 days before the war ended. Captain Tsuruno made three flights in the Shinden prototype clocking a total of only 45 minutes of flying time. This aircraft is the one pictured. A second prototype was delivered, but never flown. The turbojet-powered model, which might have solved the problems revealed in the test flights of the prototype, was still on the drawing board at war's end.

The cockpit of the J7W1 Shinden presented a clean, modern appearance with control cables and linkages hidden behind panels. The main panel was basic with the flight-control instruments clustered in the center and engine instruments to the left. The cockpit overall shows the effects of having been modified for American flight-testing after capture. The control panel has several instruments that have been either added, relocated, or are missing. One such item is the gunsight, which was mounted near the top center of the panel. Unfortunately, the poor quality of the alloy used in the structure of the aircraft is likely to make future restoration a daunting challenge.

THE SIZABLE PROTOTYPE SHINDEN BEING SURVEYED BY AN AMERICAN INTELLIGENCE TEAM.

AN EARLY-MODEL PBM TAKING OFF.

MARTIN PBM–5A MARINER

Overshadowed by the ubiquitous Consolidated PBY Catalina, the Martin PBM Mariner was, in many ways, a much more capable aircraft. Serving in both the Atlantic and Pacific theaters, the PBM performed a wide variety of missions. Although it entered service at the start of the war, it wasn't until near the end that it was available in sufficient numbers to take over most of the Catalina's duties.

In 1937, the Glenn L. Martin Company began the design of a two-engine patrol bomber for the U.S. Navy. In order to test the design without the expense of a full-size prototype, Martin built a 3/8-scale powered, man-carrying demonstration model know as the "Tadpole Clipper" (also in the National Air and Space Museum collection). Based on the successful results of these tests, a full-size aircraft was built.

The Martin patrol bomber featured a deep hull that kept the cockpit well above the sea spray. Gull-shaped wings fixed to the upper fuselage also elevated the engines above the harmful salt water. The Mariner's large hull made for an efficient workspace and crew members were positioned on a spacious flight deck high up inside the aircraft for better communication. Designed for long patrol flights, the pilot and copilot were provided with large, comfortable seats. The spacious hull provided room for more interior amenities—a galley, mess deck, and bunks for long patrol flights. A distinctive feature of the production models was the upward-canted horizontal stabilizer and large, inward-leaning vertical tails.

Accepted by the Navy in 1940, the Martin PBM Mariner was upgraded throughout the war with improved engines and armament. Several specialized versions also existed. Of some 1,300 built, this PBM–5A—an amphibious version of the aircraft including retractable landing gear for operating on land—is the only remaining example. This model entered service in late 1945 and operated during the Korean War before being retired from the U.S. Navy in 1956.

The instrument panel includes basic flight instruments on both left and right for the pilot and copilot. A navigation radar scope, which was not installed on earlier models, is visible in the center. Throttle and propeller controls are mounted between the pilots on the roof of the cockpit, simplifying linkage to the engines in the wing above. A duplicate set was mounted above the flight engineer's station. This aircraft was modified into a transport and the bomb release switches usually mounted on the spokes of the control wheel are not present.

ABOVE: NAVIGATOR'S POSITION. RIGHT: FLIGHT ENGINEER'S POSITION.

MESSERSCHMITT ME 262 A-1A SCHWALBE

The Messerschmitt Me 262 was a revolutionary aircraft. The world's first operational jet fighter, it was more than 100 mph faster than the best Allied fighters. Design of the Schwalbe (Swallow) began before the war in 1939, but progress was slow. The need for the new aircraft was not realized at the start of the war when many high-ranking officers believed conventional aircraft would achieve victory. Messerschmitt was also reluctant to impinge on the production of proven types.

The main delay in getting the Me 262 into service was the series of technical problems encountered in the development of the jet engines. The prototype first flew in April 1941 with a conventional engine. The first flight with jet engines was not made until July 1942 and nearly two more years passed before the first deliveries began in 1944.

When it finally entered combat, the Me 262 proved its advantages in speed and armament. Equipped with four 30 mm cannons, and sometimes R4M air-to-air rockets, it was a deadly opponent, but it had some liabilities that Allied pilots learned to exploit. The jet engines consumed large amounts of fuel that limited the aircraft's range. The Jumo 004 engines were sensitive to all but the smoothest changes in power, severely handicapping the Me 262 in dogfights. This made it especially vulnerable to enemy fighters when approaching to land. Allied air superiority was so great by the time the Me 262 came into service that their airfields were often under attack.

Although some 1,400 were produced, only about 300 Me 262s entered combat. Despite its promise, the Me 262 entered service too late and in too few numbers to disrupt the Allied air offensive.

This Me 262 fared better than most. It was the personal mount of Oberfeldwebel Heinz Arnold from Fighter Wing JG7, who as one of the most accomplished jet aces of the war, claimed kills of one P–47, three P–51s, and four B–17s between March 3 and March 24, 1945. Arnold was himself killed a short time later in another Me 262.

Except for the instruments and controls related to its revolutionary propulsion system, the cockpit of the Me 262 was consistent with other German fighter cockpits. Just visible on the far right is the throttle control for one of the jet engines with its push-start button. The red handle on the right rail is the emergency canopy release. The gunsight at the center top could be pivoted to the right to increase forward visibility for landing.

THE NATIONAL AIR AND SPACE MUSEUM'S "YELLOW 7" ME 262 UPON COMPLETION OF ITS EXTENSIVE RESTORATION.

MITSUBISHI A6M5 REISEN MODEL 52 "ZEKE"

In 1938, the Imperial Japanese Navy issued a specification for a new, state-of-the-art fighter that would combine maneuverability, range, and endurance. New alloys and construction techniques resulted in a light, but highly maneuverable aircraft, well armed with two 7.7 mm machine guns in the fuselage and a 20 mm cannon in each wing.

The prototype was accepted as the A6M1 Type 0 Carrier Borne Fighter. The Type 0 designation came from the Japanese calendar year 2600 (1940) in which the A6M entered service. In Japanese, the official title was shortened to Reisen (Zero Fighter). The A6M debuted in China where it faced little modern opposition. The Zero's superior performance quickly earned it a reputation of near invincibility. Its low wing loading gave it an exceptionally small turning radius and made it a deadly opponent for inexperienced pilots.

The Zero's kill tally grew rapidly in the first six months after Pearl Harbor, as did its fearsome reputation. Soon, American pilots began to hold their own against the Zero by avoiding turning fights and using advantages in speed and acceleration. With the introduction of models such as the Hellcat and Corsair, American planes decidedly outclassed the Zero in all but turning radius. While the Zero never had an engine over 1,200 horsepower, the newer American fighters were operating with 2,000 horsepower power plants. A significant liability for early Zeros was their lack of armor protection and self-sealing fuel tanks. Japanese doctrine saw the fighter as a light offensive weapon and defensive measures were seen as unnecessary.

This aircraft is an A6M5 model, introduced in 1943 in an attempt to match the performance of new American fighters. A shorter wingspan with a heavier gauge skin increased diving speed and a modified engine exhaust system increased maximum speed. The A6M5 was the most-produced model of the Zero. It could challenge midwar American fighters when flown by an experienced pilot, but Japan had very few of them left in the last years of the war.

A distinctive feature of Zero fighters was the protrusion of the nose-mounted machine guns past the instrument panel into the cockpit. In this position, the pilot could reach the cocking handles on the inboard sides of the guns and manually charge them. This eliminated the requirement for remote charging mechanisms, thus saving weight. The compass in the center of the panel has a recessed mounting so that in flight it sits level in the angled instrument panel.

A CAPTURED A6M5 UNDERGOING AMERICAN EVALUATION.

MORANE-SAULNIER M.S.500 CRIQUET

Germany's Fieseler Fi 156 Storch had an impact on military aviation far in excess of its diminutive size. Besides providing the German military with a rugged and capable liaison aircraft, it led to a complete reevaluation of the liaison and forward observation missions in other armies. Designed in 1935 as a general utility plane, its dramatic short-field performance quickly caught the attention of an international audience. Military planners were eager for an aircraft that could keep pace with new theories of maneuver warfare and replace the tethered observation balloons that had been the standard observation platform since World War I.

With a nearly 900-lb payload, and takeoff and landing distances over a 50-foot obstacle of less than 400 feet, the Storch outperformed other STOL (Short Take-Off and Landing) aircraft. The Storch served on all German fronts and is perhaps best known for the mountaintop rescue of Benito Mussolini and for serving as Rommel's eyes in the Western Desert. It was also a harbinger of defeat, being the last aircraft to fly into Berlin before its fall and the last aircraft lost in aerial combat in the European theater.

The Luftwaffe acquired nearly 3,000 Fi 156s, with about a quarter built at the Morane-Saulnier factory near Paris. After liberation, the factory continued to produce aircraft for the French military under the M.S.500 designation. This example was a wartime gift of the French government to Gen. Carl Spaatz. Though the M.S.500 saw much less employment in World War II than their German counterparts, they were used extensively in French counterinsurgency operations against the Viet Minh in Indochina during the 1950s.

With accommodation for three, the cabin of the Storch was roomy compared to the two-place American L–4 and L–5 aircraft typically used in the liaison mission. The key to the Storch's excellent low-speed handling characteristics, which allowed it to fly as slow as 31 mph, were its fixed leading-edge Handley Page slots and trailing-edge Fowler flaps. At flap settings of more than 20 degrees, the ailerons augmented them by collectively moving downward as well.

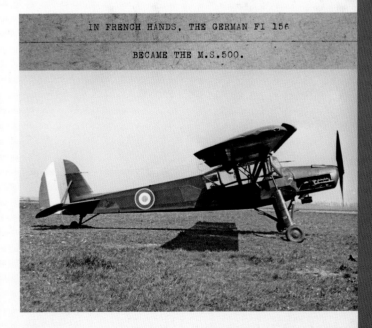

IN FRENCH HANDS, THE GERMAN FI 156

BECAME THE M.S.500.

NAKAJIMA J1N1-S GEKKO "IRVING"

American heavy bomber operations early in the Pacific War relied on the cover of darkness. The Imperial Japanese Navy moved quickly to deploy a land-based night interceptor to defend against these attacks. The result was the J1N1-S, a much-improved version of an ineffective long-range fighter and reconnaissance aircraft developed shortly before the outbreak of the Pacific War. Like Germany's Messerschmitt Me 110 night fighter conversions, the maneuverability limitations that made the Irving vulnerable during daytime fighter operations were inconsequential at night. The twin-engine J1N1-S airframe was sufficiently stable for the stealthy approach required for night bomber intercepts.

Unfortunately for the Japanese navy, the state of their airborne intercept radar was quite poor. Only in the closing days of the war were effective FD–2 airborne intercept sets fitted to the Irving. For most combat operations, the Gekko (Moonlight) depended on ground-based radars to locate targets. On approaching a target, the crew used a nose-mounted searchlight to complete the attack.

In comparison with the Northrop P–61 Black Widow, the Gekko was hopelessly outclassed. It was too slow to engage B–29s effectively. Slower B–17s and B–24s were the Gekko's preferred targets. Fewer than 500 Gekkos were constructed, but they were one of the few modestly successful countermeasures the Japanese had against nocturnal heavy bomber raids.

The Gekko featured two upward-firing oblique-mounted 20 mm cannons and two mounted to fire downward. Similar to German night fighter armament, this arrangement allowed the night fighter to move in from above or below the bomber undetected and still remain out of the lethal firing arc of the bomber's tail guns. The crews' preferred battle tactic was to approach from below as it was much easier to maintain visual contact with the target; as a result, the downward firing guns were removed. This accounts for the most obvious aspect of the J1N1's cockpit—namely the huge hole in the pilot's instrument panel, which previously mounted a Type 98 gunsight for the downward-firing 20 mm cannons. The pilot had a simple Type 3 reflecting gunsight mounted at a 30-degree angle on the top of the canopy for the dorsal upward-firing cannons. A shortage of autopilots meant most Gekkos had to operate without this highly desirable equipment. The radar operator had a swiveling seat, but none of the FD–2 radar equipment survives. Outside of the Yagi antenna on the nose, the exact placement of this hardware in the aircraft is unclear, though the radar operator would likely have been facing to the rear to view the radar oscilloscope.

THE SOLE SURVIVING GEKKO ON DISPLAY AT THE UDVAR-HAZY CENTER.

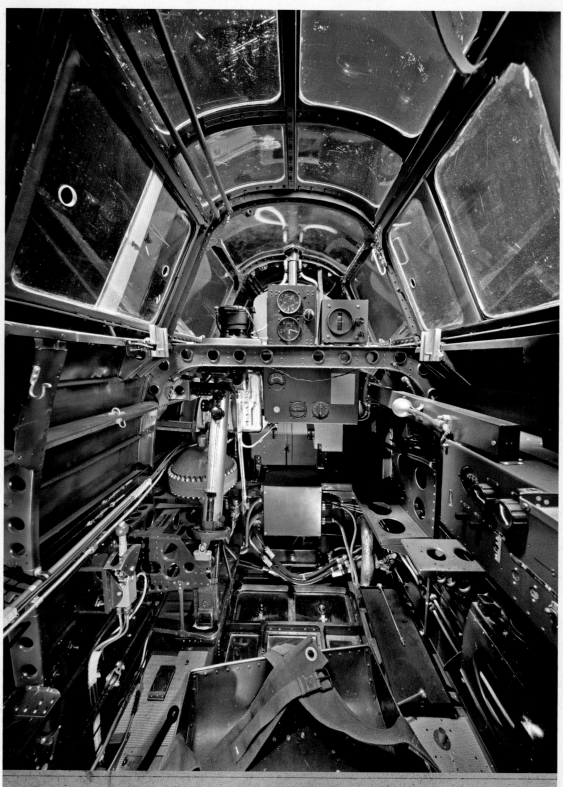

NAVIGATOR/RADAR OPERATOR'S POSITION.

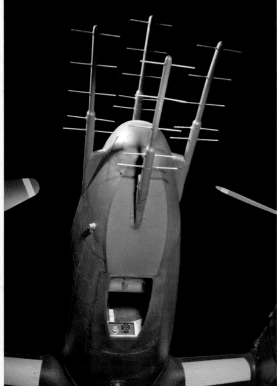

ABOVE: THE OBLIQUE FIRING CANNONS MUST HAVE DEAFENED AND BLINDED THE NAVIGATOR/RADAR OPERATOR, AS THEY FIRED IMMEDIATELY BEHIND HIS POSITION. LEFT: THE NOSE OF THIS GEKKO CONTAINED THE YAGI ANTENNAS FOR THE FD-2 RADAR. THE LARGE WINDOW HOUSED THE SIGHT FOR THE DOWNWARD-FIRING OBLIQUE ARMAMENT THAT WAS INITIALLY MOUNTED ON THE J1N1-S NIGHT FIGHTERS.

NAKAJIMA KI-115A TSURUGI

By early 1945, Japan was preparing for the Allied invasion of its home islands. A significant portion of the planned response was in the form of suicide attacks. Frontline fighter aircraft were increasingly in short supply and, like the Imperial Japanese Navy's Ohka, the army developed a disposable aircraft that was simple and easy to manufacture. The result was crude, a marginal aircraft by the standards of the time. The Tsurugi (Saber) was intended for construction by semiskilled labor in remote sites, such as schools, which were less likely to be directly targeted by American airpower.

Wooden parts stood in for metal ones. Instead of retractable landing gear, the aircraft featured crude, jettisonable main landing gear that were dropped after takeoff and a fixed tailskid. The airframe was designed to accommodate a wide range of surplus or obsolete engines that could be rapidly bolted on. The Tsurugi's sole armament consisted of an 800-kilogram bomb bolted to the underside. Provisions were also made to affix auxiliary rockets to boost the force of impact. Yet, even then, by securing the bomb to the plane, its penetrating power was far less than if the bomb was dropped ballistically, as its terminal velocity was much higher than that of the airplane. Flight tests were finished in June 1945 and more than 100 Ki-115s were completed, but none saw service. In the face of far superior American fighters and radar-directed antiaircraft guns with proximity-fused shells, attempts to employ the Tsurugi would likely have met disaster. Though intended to be used by novice pilots, the crude nature of the design and construction required a reasonably skilled aviator. By mid-1945, there were very few of those left in Japan.

This example was a prototype demonstrator. The cockpit highlights a number of unusual features. The control stick and throttle quadrant are simple constructions made out of teakwood. To the left of the seat, a simple wooden handle jettisoned the landing gear. The occluded instrument is a manifold pressure gauge and the missing vertical strip previously housed an inclinometer. The two red buttons on the left of the panel activated the auxiliary rocket units. The cockpit lacked a sliding canopy and a rudimentary dive impact sight extended from the front windscreen.

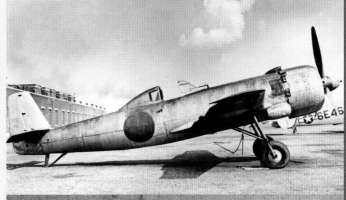

PERHAPS THE CRUDEST COMBAT AIRCRAFT OF WORLD WAR II, THE TSURUGI WAS BUILT FOR A SINGLE ONE-WAY FLIGHT.

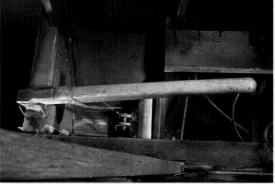

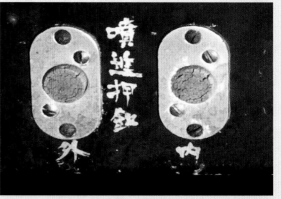

ABOVE (LEFT): THE TSURUGI'S SIMPLE TEAK CONTROL COLUMN.

ABOVE RIGHT (TOP): THIS PLAIN LEVER JETTISONED THE LANDING

GEAR ON TAKEOFF.

ABOVE RIGHT (BOTTOM): THESE BUTTONS ACTIVATED AUXILIARY DIVE

ROCKETS TO SPEED THE TSURUGI INTO ITS TARGET.

OPPOSITE (TOP): THE TSURUGI PILOT HAD ONLY THIS SIMPLE SIGHT

TO ALIGN HIS FINAL, FATAL DIVE.

OPPOSITE (BOTTOM): THIS CRUDE THROTTLE QUADRANT ONLY

HAD TO LAST FOR ONE FLIGHT.

NOORDUYN YC-64
NORSEMAN IV

Utility and cargo aircraft—the lifeblood of the logistics chain in every combat theater—are often overlooked. While the important role of C-47s and larger aircraft is well remembered, these aircraft could not operate safely from improvised landing sites in forward areas. Carrying a variety of cargo, ammunition, food, wounded troops, commanders, and other key personnel were a few of the critical missions performed by utility aircraft like the Norseman.

Designed to operate in austere conditions, Noorduyn's Norseman, manufactured in Montreal, Canada, could operate effectively with wheels, skis, or floats. It first took to the air in 1935 and was sold principally in the Canadian market. After Pearl Harbor, the Army Air Forces acquired seven Norseman IV aircraft, designated YC-64, as service test aircraft. The example seen here was one of the seven and its performance encouraged the purchase of over 700 UC-64 production aircraft.

The unheralded Norseman served widely, but evokes little interest in observers of military aircraft. One of the few occasions where its existence was noted was when famed bandleader Glenn Miller perished in one over the English Channel in December 1944. With a useful load of more than 2,500 lbs, the UC-64 could transport eight men or a spare aircraft engine, but its most significant service may have been supplying the construction of the critical Alaskan Highway. Other missions included the aerial training of navigators and radio operators, transport of rescue teams and sled dogs, and aerial surveying.

This YC-64 spent considerable time in Goose Bay, Labrador, supporting the Ferry Command and, as a result, featured specialized accommodations for that difficult environment, most notably the addition of a navigator/radio operator's station featuring a radio compass and drift sight. One important advantage of the Norseman's Canadian origins was its effective cabin-heating system. Lacking an autopilot, long periods of blind flying in the aircraft would have been tedious. This YC-64 also lacks many of the standardized military refinements present on production UC-64s, particularly in regard to the electrical panel. The search and rescue mission assigned to this aircraft is apparent. The nonstandard parachute flare dispenser in the rear of the aircraft includes a single remotely fired tube for a large flare and a triple launcher system for smaller ones.

DESIGNED FOR THE CANADIAN BACKCOUNTRY,

THE NORSEMAN WAS AT HOME ON ALMOST ANY TERRAIN.

NORTH AMERICAN O-47A

The O-47 began life as the GA-15, designed in 1935 by the General Aviation Manufacturing Company. A modern all-metal, cantilever monoplane, with hydraulic flaps and retractable undercarriage, what really made the GA-15 different from previous observation types was that it was designed for this role from the outset.

The GA-15 incorporated a large greenhouse canopy that was uncommon for the time. Located in the center of the aircraft was a seat, with duplicate flying controls, known as the auxiliary pilot's position. However, this crew member could also lower himself into the observer's position in the belly of the aircraft. In this position, he was surrounded by windows and had an unobstructed view downward to observe and photograph. This bulge in the fuselage gave the aircraft an ungainly look, but it was relatively fast and made a stable observation platform. The GA-15 was armed with a single .30 caliber gun in the right wing and another on a ring mount for the rear gunner.

In January 1936, the design was officially accepted for testing as the XO-47. About the same time, North American Aviation—the holding company that owned General Aviation—turned to manufacturing. The O-47 thus became North American's first aircraft. In August of the same year, the Air Corps issued a contract for the O-47A that was the largest for an observation type up to that time. With war looming, the modified O-47B entered service with an improved and more powerful radial engine.

The slow-flying O-47, however, was not up to the rigors of modern warfare. Even before the start of World War II, they were consistently "shot down" in war games. These exercises demonstrated that a new

TOO CUMBERSOME FOR ITS INTENDED TACTICAL RECONNAISSANCE MISSION, THE O-47 DID SUPPORT THE

CAMPAIGN AGAINST U-BOATS LURKING OFF THE AMERICAN COAST.

class of light liaison planes could better fulfill the short artillery observation role, while camera-carrying fighter and bomber conversions were more successful at long-range reconnaissance.

The large size of the O–47 provided a roomy cockpit for its pilot. The engine control quadrant was mounted so high on the left side that pilots were warned to not bend the levers while entering the cockpit. The covered N–2 gunsight was mounted on the floor just in front of the stick with its reflector glass mounted atop the glare shield. Between the stick and the right foot trough was the foot starter switch. Located on the right side panel was a black handle that, when pulled, charged the wing gun and opened a door that allowed links to be discharged.

ABOVE: THE AUXILIARY PILOT'S POSITION.

RIGHT: THE LOWER OBSERVER'S POSITION.

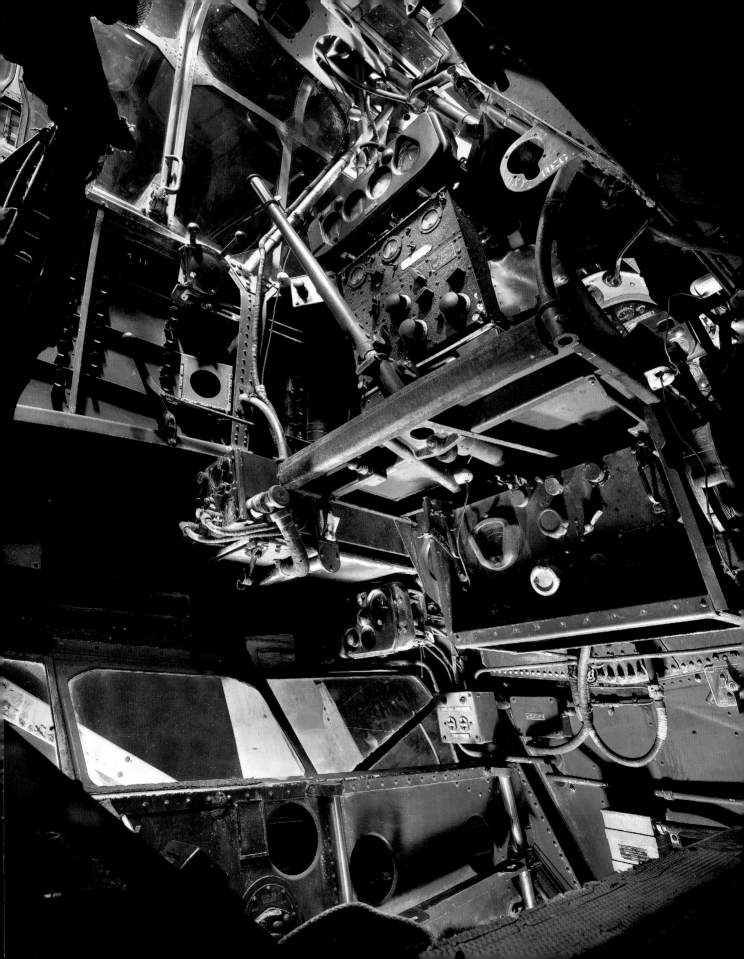

North American P-51D Mustang

In 1943, the American daylight strategic bombing campaign was in trouble. Escorting fighters did not have the range to accompany the bombers all the way to targets deep into the center of Germany. Once the escort fighters turned back, the bombers suffered terrible losses at the hands of skilled Luftwaffe pilots. A solution was desperately needed. With a little modification—the addition of auxiliary fuel tanks and a more efficient and powerful engine—the North American P-51 Mustang became the best long-range escort fighter aircraft of the war.

In 1940, British purchasing agents approached North American Aviation to build Curtiss P-40s under license. Preferring to build an original aircraft, North American proposed to design a new fighter for the British. Completed in just 117 days, the Mustang soon proved to have outstanding low-level performance. The Mustang's early success with ground-attack missions prompted the U.S. Army Air Corps to order a dive-bomber version known as the A-36. This was followed by the P-51A fighter with improved speed.

In 1942, the British began experimenting with the Rolls Royce Merlin engine in place of the original Allison to increase high-altitude performance. Encouraged by the results, North American modified the Mustang to take the Merlin engine. The new fighter was some 50 mph faster and had a ceiling of 42,000 feet. With the addition of wing drop tanks, in March 1944, Mustangs escorted U.S. bombers all the way to Berlin and back. The early Mustang's limited rearward visibility was improved by the introduction of the bubble canopy on the P-51D model. This modification resulted in the classic Mustang profile most known today.

In the center and left of the instrument panel are the six blind flying instruments. The P-51D was the first model to have them in these newly adopted standard positions. A K-14 gunsight was mounted at the top of the instrument panel (not installed here). The bomb release or rocket launch button is at the top of the control stick, while the trigger operates the machine guns and camera. The throttle handle on the left side wall has a silver remote transmit-receive switch so that the pilot could operate the radio without taking his hand off the controls. On the right side is the control for the AN/APS-13 tail warning radar. The round object at the top left of the instrument glare shield is the warning light for this system. This light, combined with a bell, warned the pilot of aircraft approaching from the rear.

LT. VERNON L. RICHARDS OF THE 374TH FIGHTER GROUP, 361ST FIGHTER SQUADRON AT THE CONTROLS OF *TIKA IV* IN THE SKIES OVER ENGLAND.

NORTH AMERICAN SNJ-4 TEXAN

With the advent of high-performance monoplane fighters in the 1930s, the gap between simple primary trainers and operational aircraft widened. What was needed was an advanced trainer that would allow student pilots to experience high performance while still being forgiving of novices' mistakes. The North American AT-6/SNJ Texan was perfect for the job. It was purchased or built under contract by more than 40 different countries leading to the production of nearly 15,000 examples.

In 1935, newly named North American Aviation decided to submit a design to the Army's basic trainer competition. The NA-16 easily won the competition and was accepted for production. Originally designated the BT-9 (NJ-1 in Navy service), several modifications to Army and Navy specifications ensued. Production was finally standardized between the two services and the AT-6A and SNJ-3 became nearly interchangeable. One of the only variations was that the SNJ-3C included a tail hook for carrier training.

With orders pouring in, North American opened a second plant in Dallas, Texas, in 1941. Most of the AT-6/SNJs were built at this plant and this contributed to the plane being named the Texan. Several export versions were built, including one for the British known as the Harvard. The Texan was also manufactured in Australia as the Wirraway.

Scheduled for retirement at the end of World War II, the lack of a suitable trainer replacement during the Korean War meant that the Texan was recalled for a second tour of duty. Because of its ease of operation and plentiful numbers, the Texan continues to be popular among aerobatic, racing, and war-bird enthusiasts, appearing at air shows all over the world.

SNJ-4s, like this aircraft, were the first of the naval Texans to carry a wing-mounted machine gun and provisions for underwing bomb racks. The bomb release button can be seen at the top of the control stick. The large panel to the lower left of the main instrument panel is the electrical control panel, with the parking brake handle just below on the right side. Preflight (right) and takeoff and landing (left) checklists have been affixed to the instrument panel. The right side of the cockpit contains the radio equipment.

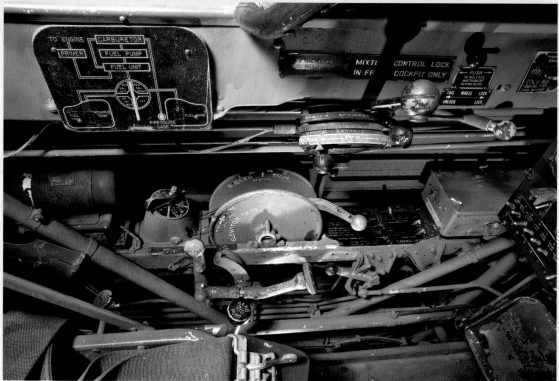

ABOVE: COMMANDER DONALD F. SMITH TAKES AVIATION MACHINISTS'

MATE 1ST CLASS HAROLD DIETZ FOR A RIDE IN 1941.

OPPOSITE ABOVE: THE NATIONAL AIR-AND SPACE MUSEUM'S SNJ-4

IN STORAGE AT THE PAUL E. GARBER FACILITY.

OPPOSITE BOTTOM: DETAIL OF THE UNRESTORED PILOT'S

THROTTLE QUADRANT.

NORTHROP P-61C BLACK WIDOW

The devastating German Blitz against London convinced the Army Air Corps to develop a night fighter capable of localized defense against nocturnal bombers. Design began in late 1940 and the prototype XP-61 took to the air in May 1942, but was not operationally deployed until mid–1944.

The P-61 was principally a flying platform for its radar and gun systems. The Western Electric SCR-720 radar had an intercept range of nearly five miles. A GCI (Ground Control Intercept) radar operator talked the pilot toward his target. Once the radar operator, who sat facing rearward in his own compartment in the tail, picked up the target on the SCR-720, he directed the pilot into a firing position behind and below the enemy plane. When in position, the P-61's gunner, sitting in a raised tandem seat behind the pilot, engaged the target visually with a gun turret that allowed offset targeting without the pilot having to move into position directly behind the enemy aircraft. This configuration provided a considerable advantage over Axis night fighters, such as the Japanese Irving that had only fixed oblique-firing armament.

The Black Widow carried a devastating array of armament, including four 20 mm cannons in an underbelly gondola and a turret with four .50 caliber machine guns. In addition to the destruction of a number of Fi 103 (V–1) German flying bombs, P-61s accounted for 127 enemy fighters in aerial combat, of which 69 were Japanese.

This P-61, like all "C" models, did not see wartime service, though it had an unusual postwar career participating in Project Thunderstorm to research the hazards of convective weather, including the use of radar to avoid it. Later, it flew for the National Advisory Committee for Aeronautics (NACA) experimentations where it dropped swept-wing model shapes in free-fall tests.

The cockpit is tight for a heavy multi-engine aircraft. It differs somewhat from combat examples as it lacks the gunsight for the cannons, the SCR-695 IFF transponder that identified itself to Allied radar-equipped aircraft and ground stations, and the control box for the AN/APS-13 rear-warning radar, which could detect aircraft approaching from the rear at up to 800 yards. The pilot and gunner entered the aircraft through the top canopies, but the twin tails mandated a cumbersome bailout procedure through an escape hatch in the floor, then through the nose gear wheel well, so that before bailing out, the pilot had to lower the landing gear.

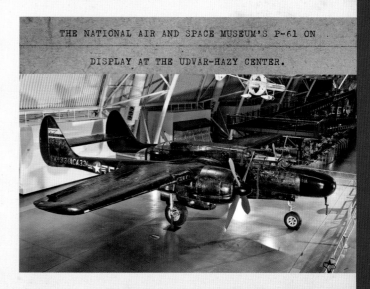

THE NATIONAL AIR AND SPACE MUSEUM'S P-61 ON DISPLAY AT THE UDVAR-HAZY CENTER.

SIKORSKY XR-5

The development of the operational military helicopter in the United States was closely intertwined with the war against U-boats in the Battle of the Atlantic. Great Britain, desperate to staunch the shipping losses, looked to a number of previously radical notions to improve air cover over convoys, including the use of rotorcraft. One of the principle officers in the British Air Commission guiding the purchase of Lend-Lease aircraft for Britain was Reginald Brie, who had an extensive background in the autogiro industry. After observing the trials of the Vought-Sikorsky XR-4 in 1942, he became an ardent proponent of employing helicopters as antisubmarine platforms. At that moment, the Army Air Forces was still pondering the value of investing large sums in large-scale helicopter development. Brie's urgent request for hundreds of antisubmarine helicopters pushed the United States into endorsing an ambitious helicopter development plan with a production target of nearly 1,500 helicopters. The most capable helicopter selected for production was the R-5, which was to form the centerpiece of the shipboard antisubmarine program. Whereas the R-4 was principally a trainer, the R-5 was to be a true utility aircraft. It could deliver ordnance in the form of depth bombs, carry wounded on the battlefield or lay pipes and critical infrastructure in jungles and difficult terrain where the United States was struggling to build new forward airfields.

Unfortunately, the R-5 was much larger than Sikorsky's previous helicopter efforts and posed a host of new engineering challenges that severely delayed the program, but by more than doubling the useful load of the R-4, the R-5 represented the advent of the helicopter as a practical tool for the battlefield. Unfortunately, the first operational examples were not ready for acceptance until the last days of the war with Japan. Postwar, the R-5 series saw extensive service in the United States and abroad with improved versions experiencing combat in Korea, Malaya, and Indochina, where they saved thousands of lives.

On the XR-5 and the R-5A production models, the observer/bombardier sat in the front with an exceptional view (like a modern attack helicopter), while the pilot sat behind with a considerably more obstructed perspective. Up to four litter "pods" attached to external beams mounted adjacent to the engine accommodated wounded soldiers. By war's end, the idea of using this helicopter type for bombing had faded away and on subsequent models, the pilot moved to the front and the rear cabin was widened to accommodate three passengers.

THE NATIONAL AIR AND SPACE MUSEUM'S XR-5 LOADED WITH DEPTH BOMBS, 1944.

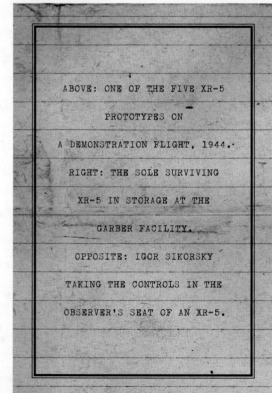

ABOVE: ONE OF THE FIVE XR-5

PROTOTYPES ON

A DEMONSTRATION FLIGHT, 1944.

RIGHT: THE SOLE SURVIVING

XR-5 IN STORAGE AT THE

GARBER FACILITY.

OPPOSITE: IGOR SIKORSKY

TAKING THE CONTROLS IN THE

OBSERVER'S SEAT OF AN XR-5.

SUPERMARINE SPITFIRE HF MK VII

No other aircraft symbolizes Britain's efforts to fight on in the face of seemingly impossible odds in the early years of the war like the Supermarine Spitfire. Although not as plentiful during the Battle of Britain as its counterpart the Hawker Hurricane, the Spitfire would come to be forever associated with that struggle. Unlike other aircraft, which gained fame only in the early part of the war, the Spitfire would continue to be developed and was an effective fighter until the war ended.

Designed by the legendary Reginald Mitchell, who had created the sleek seaplanes that captured the Schneider Trophy in the 1930s, the Spitfire was the result of Britain's efforts to develop a modern, all-metal monoplane fighter to counter the new German aircraft. Mitchell's design featured a distinctive elliptical wing that reduced drag and increased maneuverability. When fitted with the new Rolls Royce Merlin engine, the Spitfire would exhibit outstanding performance. Improved Merlin (and later Griffon) engines would allow the Spitfire to keep pace with newer designs and remain effective.

Along with increasingly more powerful engines, the Spitfire would receive other upgrades. Armament would increase from eight .303 caliber machine guns to assortments of cannons and guns. Various modifications of the basic airframe were carried out including the addition of drop tanks to extend range and a bubble canopy to increase visibility in later models.

In 1943, a high-altitude fighter version, which featured extended wingtips, a four-bladed propeller, and a pressurized cockpit, was designed. It was designated the HF Mk VII. Only 140 examples of this variant were built, including this example. It was shipped directly from the factory to the United States in 1943 for evaluation.

The Spitfire cockpit, in common with many fighters, was a tight fit. Entry was made even more difficult on the HF Mk VII by the elimination of the small side door to facilitate cockpit pressurization. In the center of the instrument panel is the blind flying panel containing the basic six flying instruments. Introduced in the 1930s, this standard panel was unique to the RAF for most of the war. The Spitfire control column moved fully fore and aft, but because of the narrow confines of the cockpit was hinged just below the spade grip to avoid hitting the legs of the pilot. The grip holds the silver cannon and machine gun firing control at the top, a red camera button at the bottom, and the brake lever just visible in the rear.

THE NATIONAL AIR AND SPACE MUSEUM'S SPITFIRE VII WAS EVALUATED BY THE ARMY AIR FORCES AND THE NATIONAL ADVISORY COMMITTEE FOR AERONAUTICS.

VOUGHT-SIKORSKY OS2U-3 KINGFISHER

Perched on a catapult at the stern of a battleship, the OS2U Kingfisher symbolized a passing era where the big guns of the battleships and cruisers were viewed as the main offensive weapon and aircraft served a support role. Used for scouting ahead of the fleet, spotting for naval gunnery and rescue operations, the Kingfisher's duties as the eyes of the fleet were eventually superseded by radar. The OS2U, however, took on new duties and was to be present at the Japanese surrender at Tokyo Bay, just as it had been during the initial attack at Pearl Harbor.

In the mid-1930s, the U.S. Navy's efforts to replace its biplane aircraft led to the award of a contract to Vought Aircraft for a new all-metal monoplane observation-scout plane. The new design included many revolutionary features. Spot welding created a smooth, nonbuckling fuselage while full-wingspan flaps and spoilers were incorporated to aid in slow-speed handling. Munitions included both conventional high explosive and depth bombs mounted under the wings. The Kingfisher could operate either as a floatplane or with conventional landing gear from land-based runways. By the time the OS2U Kingfisher entered service in 1940, Vought had been merged with Sikorsky as subsidiaries of United Aircraft and production commenced under the combined name.

This aircraft is the OS2U-3 version—the most-produced variant. It differed from its predecessor through the addition of extra fuel tanks, increased armor for the crew, and a more powerful engine. On July 4, 1944, Lt. (jg) Roland Batten won the Navy Cross while flying this aircraft during the rescue of two downed naval aviators.

The location of the Kingfisher's front cockpit immediately signals that its primary duty is observation. Its position ahead of the leading edge of the large wing affords the pilot a clear downward view while the low cockpit rails increase visibility and roominess. Although an observation aircraft, the OS2U was armed with a single .30 caliber machine gun in both the front and rear. The ammo box for the forward gun is visible in front of the stick between the rudder pedals. Although not installed on this aircraft, the gun would normally be located just to the right of the ammo boxes. A telescopic sight is located at the top of the instrument panel and a gun camera is visible just outside the right-hand windscreen.

THE NATIONAL AIR AND SPACE MUSEUM'S OS2U-3

UPON COMPLETION OF ITS RESTORATION.

ABOVE: THE KINGFISHER ALSO PERFORMED LAND-BASED OBSERVATION MISSIONS

USING WHEELED LANDING GEAR.

ABOVE: THE KINGFISHER LAUNCHED FROM BATTLESHIPS AND CRUISERS USING

A GUNPOWDER-POWERED CATAPULT.

BELOW: TO RECOVER THE KINGFISHER, ITS VESSEL DEPLOYED A TOWED MAT.

THE KINGFISHER PILOT WOULD TAXI ONTO THE MAT WHERE A HOOK ON THE BOTTOM OF

THE FLOAT WOULD CATCH THE MAT AND HOLD THE AIRCRAFT FAST. THEN,

A DECK CRANE WOULD LIFT THE KINGFISHER BACK ONTO THE CATAPULT.

THE XR-4 DEMONSTRATES PRACTICAL SHIPBOARD OPERATIONS, MAY 1943 (LEFT). THE R-4'S UNGAINLY

(BUT FUNCTIONAL) ROTOR HEAD (RIGHT).

VOUGHT-SIKORSKY XR-4C

The R-4 was the first helicopter to go into full-scale production and enter regular military service. The prototype XR-4 made its first flight on January 14, 1942, and quickly demonstrated that it could serve as an effective trainer and demonstrator for the widespread introduction of helicopters to military service. In May 1942, it flew 761 miles from Stratford, Connecticut, to Wright Field, Ohio, where it became the first helicopter to be accepted by the military. The Army Air Forces put the XR-4 through its paces with an eye toward combating the U-boat menace in the Atlantic where they could give convoying merchant vessels a modicum of air cover. Trials included dropping depth bombs, deploying hydrophones, and landing on a ship's deck.

By mid-1943, the XR-4 had established the type's viability and three YR-4As, twenty-six YR-4Bs, and one hundred R-4Bs were being delivered or were about to enter production. The R-4 never had the opportunity to confront U-boats. Eighteen made it to the Burma and Pacific theaters where they rescued nearly 100 injured and wounded personnel between April 1944 and the war's end, though the type's primary use was as a trainer for improved types.

Early helicopter operations were undertaken only in daylight and fair weather, so the instrument panel did not incorporate any gyroscopic instruments. The useful load of the R-4 was marginal and a single passenger/student and a partial fuel load were about all the aircraft could lift in typical flight conditions. Radios, if installed at all, were mounted in the back of the cockpit and were unreachable in flight, which meant that frequencies had to be set correctly beforehand.

An unusual feature of the R-4 was that unlike later helicopter trainers, it had only one collective pitch lever and throttle, located between the seats (for mechanical simplicity). With helicopter control depending on constant cyclic inputs, right-handed pilots wanted to leave their left hand free for the collective lever as it required far less manipulation. This meant that students in the R-4 had to learn from the right seat rather than from the left as was traditional for an airplane pilot. As the R-4 was the primary helicopter trainer through World War II, the first generation of helicopter pilots in the United States and Great Britain adopted a right-seat convention for helicopter piloting—a tradition that has largely held to the present day.

PHOTOGRAPHY CREDITS

FOCKE-WULF FW 190 D–9
78 SI 2009–12426 **79** SI 2009–12425

FOCKE-WULF FW 190 F–8
80 SI 2009–12381 **81** SI 2005–35239 (LEFT)
81 SI 2009–12383 (RIGHT)

ILYUSHIN IL–2 SHTURMOVIK
82 SI 2001–133 **83** COURTESY OF VON HARDESTY
84 COURTESY OF VON HARDESTY **85** SI 2009–12501

KAWANISHI N1K2-JA SHIDEN KAI "GEORGE"
86 SI 2009–12433 **87** SI 2009–12427

KELLETT XO–60
88 SI 2009–12392 **89** SI 88–12578 **90** SI 2009–12487
91 SI 2009–12488

KUGISHO MXY7 OHKA MODEL 22
92 SI 2009–12403 **93** SI 2005–35866

KYUSHU J7W1 SHINDEN
94 SI 2009–12406 **95** SI 2009–9041

MARTIN PBM–5A MARINER
96 SI 2009–12422 **97** SI 2009–12031c
98 SI 2009–12420 **99** SI 2009–12394

MESSERSCHMITT ME 262 A–1A
100 SI 2009–12397 **101** SI 2001–1873

MITSUBISHI A6M5 REISEN MODEL 52 "ZEKE"
102 SI 2009–12443 **103** SI 2009–12010

MORANE-SAULNIER M.S.500 CRIQUET (FIESELER FI 156 C–7 STORCH)
104 SI 2009–12423 **105** SI 76–17753

NAKAJIMA J1N1-S GEKKO "IRVING"
106 SI 2009–12389 **107** SI 2009–12429 **108** SI 2009–12390
109 SI 2009–12391 (TOP) **109** SI 2009–12494 (BOTTOM)

NAKAJIMA KI–115A TSURUGI
110 SI 2009–12416 **111** SI 82–690 **112** SI 2009–12439 (LEFT)
112 SI 2009–12240 (TOP) **112** SI 2009–12437 (BOTTOM)
113 SI 2009–12441 (TOP) **113** SI 2009–12438 (BOTTOM)

NOORDUYN YC–64 NORSEMAN IV
114 SI 2009–12434 **115** SI 2009–9040 (COURTESY OF NOORDUYN INC.)

NORTH AMERICAN O–47A
116 SI 2009–12401 **117** SI 2009–9046 (RUDY ARNOLD PHOTO COLLECTION)
118 SI 2009–12402 **119** SI 2009–12435

NORTH AMERICAN P–51D MUSTANG
120 SI 2009–12436 **121** SI 98–15407

NORTH AMERICAN SNJ–4 TEXAN
122 SI 2009–12409 **123** SI 2009–12270 **124** SI 2009–12411 (TOP)
124 SI 2009–12410 (BOTTOM) **125** SI 2009–12032 (RUDY ARNOLD
PHOTO COLLECTION)

NORTHROP P–61C BLACK WIDOW
126 SI 2009–12404 **127** SI 2006–10364

SIKORSKY XR–5
128 SI 2009–12376 **129** SI 84–2759 **130** SI 2009–12005
(RUDY ARNOLD PHOTO COLLECTION) **131** SI 2009–12004 (RUDY ARNOLD
PHOTO COLLECTION) (TOP) **131** SI 2009–12377

SUPERMARINE SPITFIRE HF MK VII
132 SI 2009–12424 **133** SI 93–8430

VOUGHT-SIKORSKY OS2U–3 KINGFISHER
134 SI 2009–12393 **135** SI 88–10739 **136** SI 2009–12445
137 NATIONAL ARCHIVES 80-GK 1946 (TOP)
137 NATIONAL ARCHIVES 80-GK 1954 (BOTTOM)

VOUGHT-SIKORSKY XR–4C
138 SI 2009–12375 **139** SI 2009–12033 (LEFT)
139 SI 2009–30241 (LEFT)

PHOTOGRAPHY CREDITS
140 SI 2009–12031c **141** SI 2009–12418

ACKNOWLEDGMENTS
142 SI 2009–12486

ALL IMAGES ARE COURTESY OF THE NATIONAL AIR AND SPACE
MUSEUM, SMITHSONIAN INSTITUTION, EXCEPT AS NOTED.

FROM LEFT TO RIGHT: ROGER D. CONNOR, CHRISTOPHER T. MOORE, MARK A. AVINO, AND ERIC F. LONG.

ACKNOWLEDGMENTS

Eric, Mark, Roger, and Chris would like to thank the following individuals for their extraordinary efforts in support of this book.

Special recognition must go to Dane Penland, for shooting most of the spectacular exterior photos of the aircraft on display at the Steven F. Udvar-Hazy Center. Many of these aircraft required extensive preparation and treatment prior to photography, and we are grateful to the many hours expended by Steven Kautner, Jeff Mercer, and John Shatz over the course of the project.

The marshaling of resources is dependent on effective administration and we would like to thank Museum Director John Dailey, Deputy Director Dr. Peter Jakab, Collections Division Chief Elizabeth Garcia, Preservation and Restoration Unit Chief Richard Kowalczyk, Communications Director Claire Brown, Public Affairs Specialist Brian Mullen, and Aeronautics Chair Dr. F. Robert van der Linden.

Most of the archival images and period reference materials were provided and managed by the Archives Division and we must especially thank Jessamyn Lloyd, Brian Nicklas, Melissa Keiser, Kate Igoe, Mark Kahn, David Schwartz, and Larry Wilson.

We would like to recognize the valuable curatorial insights and review provided by Aeronautics Curators Dr. Dik Daso, Thomas Dietz, Dr. Von Hardesty, Dr. Jeremy Kinney, and Russell Lee.

Interns and volunteers are essential to Smithsonian projects and we must acknowledge the work of Matthew Breitbart, Sheralyn Morehouse, Thomas Paone, Laszlo Taba, Ciara Richards, Larry DiRicco, and Mike Hanz.

This book benefited from the support of Ellen Nanney at Smithsonian Business Ventures and Caroline Newman at SI Books. Without Trish Graboske, our ever-reliable and much beloved Publications Officer, this project would not have been possible.

We would also like to thank Matthew Nazzaro, RAD Specialist; Malcolm Collum, Chief Conservator; and Wayne Cozzolino, Calumet Photographic, and Charles Hyman, color production.

We are indebted to the staff at HarperCollins Publishers that took our raw content and turned it into the polished product you see before you, especially Marta Schooler, Elizabeth Viscott Sullivan, Signe Bergstrom, Iris Shih, and Agnieszka Stachowicz.

As a top fighter pilot, test pilot, airshow performer, and all-around nice guy, we are humbled and honored that Bob Hoover was able to write the Foreword to our book.

Completing a project of this scale is never easy and we must thank our families and especially Kathy, Laurie, and Nancy for the nights, weekends, and vacations that were sacrificed.